PSYCHO/... ... ...
PSYCHOTHERAPY AFTER
CHILD ABUSE

The Treatment of Adults and
Children Who Have Experienced
Sexual Abuse, Violence, and
Neglect in Childhood

Daniel McQueen, Roger Kennedy,
Valerie Sinason, and Fay Maxted

KARNAC

First published in 2008 by
Karnac Books Ltd
118 Finchley Road, London NW3 5HT

British Library Cataloguing in Publication Data

A C.I.P. for this book is available from the British Library

ISBN: 978 1 85575 639 7

Edited, designed and produced by The Studio Publishing Services Ltd
www.publishingservicesuk.co.uk
e-mail: studio@publishingservicesuk.co.uk

Printed in Great Britain

www.karnacbooks.com

PSYCHOANALYTIC PSYCHOTHERAPY AFTER CHILD ABUSE

CONTENTS

ACKNOWLEDGEMENTS

This guideline is the product of collaboration between a wide number of individuals and organizations concerned about the effects of child abuse and neglect, and the challenges of providing timely, appropriate, and effective therapeutic help.

The group responsible for developing this guideline was convened by Catherine Itzin, working at the Department of Health as Director of the Victims of Violence and Abuse Prevention Programme, and Policy Lead on Sexual Violence and Human Trafficking and on Domestic and Sexual Violence and Abuse. Roger Kennedy, as President of the British Psychoanalytical Society, was invited to chair the group. Susie Orbach, Professor of Sociology at the London School of Economics, co-chaired the group. Experts on child abuse and psychotherapy were invited from many fields: experts by experience, survivor groups, academics, activists, and clinicians (including paediatricians, physicians, child and adult psychiatrists, psychoanalysts, psychologists, and psychoanalytic psychotherapists). The Guideline was written after four meetings of the group and copious exchanges of e-mail.

Some individuals involved in this project stand out as deserving of special acknowledgement: Catherine Itzin, whose vision created the opportunity for these guidelines to be developed; Roger Kennedy, whose diplomatic chairmanship enabled the different voices to be heard and steered the project to completion; Susie Orbach, for co-chairing the group; Valerie Sinason, Director of the Clinic for Dissociative Studies, who ensured that victims of abuse at risk of being forgotten were not overlooked; Fay Maxted, Chief Executive of the Survivors' Trust, who enabled the views of a huge number of survivor organizations to be represented; and Daniel McQueen, Specialist Registrar in Psychotherapy at the Cassel Hospital Family Service, who had the task of writing the Guideline and reconciling the different views. Thanks are due for the invaluable written contributions received from Gillian Finch, Tirril Harris, Kathryn Livingston, Mary Target, Margaret Wilkinson, and Felicity de Zulueta. It would not have been possible to produce this Guideline without the thoughtful contributions of all of the members of the Guideline Development Group.

Finally, thanks are due to the Department of Health for the generous financial support that made this publication possible.

ABOUT THE AUTHORS

Daniel McQueen obtained degrees in medicine and psychology from Sheffield University Medical School. He worked in general medicine, and as a General Practitioner before training in psychiatry. He works as a Specialist Registrar Psychiatrist in Psychotherapy on the Family Unit and Emerging and Severe Personality Disorder Unit at the Cassel Hospital, and Psychotherapy Service at West Middlesex University Hospital.

Roger Kennedy is Consultant Psychiatrist at the Family Unit of the Cassel Hospital, an Honorary Senior Lecturer in Psychiatry at Imperial College London, and Past President of the British Psychoanalytical Society. He is the author of ten books, including *Psychotherapists as Expert Witnesses* (2005), and *The Many Voices of Psychoanalysis* (2007).

Valerie Sinason PhD is a poet, writer, child and adult psychotherapist, and adult psychoanalyst. She is Director of the Clinic for Dissociative Studies. She is an Honorary Consultant to the Child Guidance Clinic at the University of Cape Town and President of the Institute for Psychotherapy and Disability. She has been a consultant child psychotherapist at the Tavistock Clinic and a consultant research psychoanalyst at the Department of Disability Psychiatry at St Georges Hospital Medical School. She specializes in trauma and disability and has authored eleven books, written many papers, and contributed chapters to a number of edited volumes. She edited *Attachment, Trauma and Multiplicity: Working with Dissociative Identity Disorder* (2002).

Fay Maxted is Chief Executive of The Survivors Trust, an umbrella agency for specialist voluntary sector services for rape and childhood sexual abuse. She represents The Survivors Trust on a range of advisory groups and committees, including The National Stakeholder Advisory Group on Sexual Violence and Abuse, the Stop It Now! UK and Ireland Advisory Group, the ACPO Rape Working Group, and Expert Groups on Adult Survivors of Sexual Violence and Adult Survivors of Childhood Sexual Abuse for the joint Home Office and Department of Health Victims of Violence and Abuse Prevention Programme. She is a volunteer supervisor and trainer with Rugby RoSA, a rape crisis and sexual abuse counselling service, and has been involved in the development and delivery of training for their counselling, helpline, and support workers over the past twelve years. She is also co-author, with Robert Kelly, of *The Survivor's Guide to Recovery from Rape or Sexual Abuse*, a self-help book designed to be accessible for all victims of sexual violence from the age of twelve years.

THE GUIDELINE DEVELOPMENT GROUP

Convenor

Prof Catherine Itzin: Director, Victims of Violence and Abuse Prevention Programme, Department of Health Policy Lead on Sexual Violence and Human Trafficking and on Domestic and Sexual Violence and Abuse, Professor of Mental Health Policy at the University of Lincoln.

Co-chairs

Dr Roger Kennedy: President, British Psychoanalytical Society & Consultant Psychiatrist Cassel Hospital

Professor Susie Orbach: United Kingdom Council for Psychotherapy, British Psychoanalytical Council & London School of Economics.

Members of the Guideline Development Group

Dr Roxane Agnew-Davies: Senior Research Fellow, Institute of Primary Care and Public Health.

Camila Batmanghelidjh:	Director, Kids Company.
Sally Berry:	Arbours Association.
Maggie Brennan:	Research development and strategy adviser: Centre for Exploitation and Online Protection (CEOP).
Ann Byrne:	Women's Therapy Centre.
Dr Robert Clacey:	The Severn Institute for Psychotherapy.
Cynthia Diacre:	The Lincoln Clinic and Centre for Psychotherapy.
Dr Ronald Doctor:	Chairman, Association for Psychoanalytic Psychotherapy in the NHS.
Deirdre Dowling:	Association for Child Psychotherapists (ACP) & Cassel Hospital.
Gillian Finch:	CIS'ters (Childhood Incest Survivors).
Liz Green:	NSPCC.
Tirril Harris:	Research Fellow, Community Psychiatry, Health Service and Population Research, Institute of Psychiatry & London Centre for Psychotherapy.
Dr Daphne Keen:	Royal College of Paediatrics and Child Health.
Kathryn Livingston:	First Person Plural.
Fay Maxted:	Chief Executive, The Survivors' Trust.
Elise Ormerod:	The British Association of Psychotherapists.
Dr Karen Rogstad:	Royal College of Physicians (London) & Consultant Physician in Genitourinary Medicine, Sheffield Teaching Hospitals Foundation Trust.
Dr Valerie Sinason:	Director, Clinic for Dissociative Studies.
Mary Target PhD:	Professional Director Anna Freud Centre & Reader in Psychoanalysis University College London.
Dr Judith Trowell:	Tavistock and Portman Clinic & British Psychoanalytical Society.
Margaret Wilkinson:	The Society of Analytical Psychology.

Dr Felicity de Zulueta: Traumatic Stress Service, South London and Maudsley NHS Trust & Institute of Psychiatry.

Dr Morris Zwi: CAMHS Professional Adviser (Research), Department of Health, Partnerships for Children, Families & Maternity Services.

Main author
Dr Daniel McQueen: Specialist Registrar in Psychotherapy, Cassel Hospital.

PREFACE

It is difficult to imagine that 100 years ago the sexual abuse of children was a taboo subject. Recent decades have seen an explosion of research into the extent of child abuse and into the effects of early relational trauma on the developing mind and brain of children. The lasting effects on survivors are increasingly recognized and can be addressed psychotherapeutically, if the abuse is recognized, and if the psychotherapeutic resources are available.

Of course, there is much further to go. Stigma, guilt, and shame have not gone away, and victims still may experience disbelief. Therapeutic resources are often insufficient or simply unavailable in many parts of this country.

This guideline is unique in bringing together such a wide range of different kinds of evidence and so many different viewpoints and voices. We have striven to provide enough depth to make this into a coherent and readable narrative review of the current state of knowledge of the effects and role of psychoanalytic psychotherapy in the treatment of children and adults who have experienced childhood abuse and neglect.

Introduction

Psychoanalytic psychotherapy is one of many possible treatments proven to be helpful to people who have experienced sexual and physical abuse and neglect in their childhood.

It has not proved possible to predict reliably who will respond to which specific psychotherapy. Different individuals will be able to benefit from different approaches and treatments at different stages of their lives, depending on their wishes, circumstances, level of support, and need.

There is considerable scientific evidence of effectiveness and a considerable body of accumulated clinical experience using psychoanalytical approaches in the treatment of people who have experienced childhood sexual, physical, and emotional abuse and neglect. This guideline brings together this evidence for the first time.

There is a strong case for funding specific projects to look in more detail at the psychoanalytic psychotherapy approach to working with people who have experienced childhood trauma. Psychoanalytic psychotherapies can be integrated into a stepped care approach to the treatment of people who have experienced sexual and physical abuse and neglect in their childhood.

Purpose of this guideline

This guideline covers the use of psychoanalytic psychotherapies in the treatment and care of individuals who have experienced sexual and associated abuse and neglect in their childhood. We do not address the place of other, non-psychoanalytic, psychotherapies here.

It highlights the treatment and care needs of victims and survivors of childhood sexual and other associated abuse and neglect from a psychoanalytic perspective. It covers children, adolescents, and adults.

The guideline is intended for practitioners of psychiatric, psychological, and psychoanalytic therapies and providers of other health and mental health services.

This guideline should inform Primary Care Trusts, Children's Services commissioners, and health service providers about theoretical approaches and therapeutic practice involved in psychoanalytic psychotherapies and approaches.

This guideline describes some key features of the damage caused by childhood sexual and other associated abuse and neglect; the importance of attachment disorders (Dozier, Stovall, & Albus, 1999; Greenberg, 1999), the importance of transference as an obstacle and tool in the treatment of individuals who have been abused as children (transference describes the feelings that originate in an early relationship, usually with a parent, but which have been transferred to a current, psychotherapeutic, relationship. For further details, see Malan (2004) and Gabbard [2005], and the nature and quality of therapeutic relationships and processes).

What is psychoanalytic psychotherapy?

Psychoanalytic psychotherapy involves a therapist listening to the individual's experiences. This gives the individual an opportunity to enter into their past, to revisit feelings from past relationships and experiences, and to re-evaluate how these past relationships and experiences have shaped their life and continue to influence and perhaps seriously distort their feelings, actions, and relationships in the present. In this way the individual is able to become aware of aspects of themselves about which they may previously have been unaware.

Different psychotherapists have different styles of working. Some will take the lead and ask questions, while others will follow the patient's train of thought. Psychoanalytic psychotherapy can continue for one or several years, or may be shorter term. Psychoanalytic psychotherapy may take place one-to-one, with couples, families, or in groups. It usually takes place one or more times per week, but can occur less frequently.

Psychoanalytic psychotherapy can be especially useful in helping people with long-term or recurring problems to get to the root of their difficulties and, through understanding, to change destructive ways of relating to themselves and others.

Children express their emotional difficulties through their play and behaviour. Child psychotherapists work with children through exploring the meaning of the children's behaviour and play in the therapeutic sessions to help them put their distress into words. This helps to reduce the effects of trauma and emotional difficulties on children's further emotional development, and can help to get their emotional development back on course.

After abuse has occurred, the child therapist has an important role in supporting parents and carers to respond sensitively to children's distress. This can be vital in helping parents and carers manage their children's behaviour safely, so the children do not put themselves at further risk.

Government policy context

In response to the high prevalence of domestic violence, sexual violence, and abuse, and the evidence of resulting mental and physical ill health, the Department of Health and National Institute for Mental Health in England jointly established the Victims of Violence and Abuse Prevention Programme in 2004.

This guideline is one of the publications produced as part of the Victims of Violence and Abuse Prevention Programme. The Programme builds on the literature on the nature, extent, and effects of child sexual abuse, domestic violence, rape and sexual assault, and sexual exploitation, and its co-occurrence across these groups. The programme also covers stalking, sexual harassment, forced marriage, female genital mutilation, and "honour crime".

The purpose of the programme is to ensure that services and professionals in all sectors and settings are equipped to identify and to respond to the needs of those whose mental and physical health has been affected by domestic and sexual violence and abuse (Itzin, 2006).

The Victims of Violence and Abuse Prevention Programme conducted a Delphi Expert Consultation that included responses from 285 organizations comprising: professional bodies, independent and voluntary organizations, and survivor organizations. In considering therapeutic and treatment interventions aimed at healing or ameliorating the effects of violence or abuse, or at directly modifying violent or abusive behaviour, the Delphi Expert Consultation found that:

- Behavioural and cognitive approaches on their own are viewed as insufficient to meet the needs of children, adolescents or adults who had experienced childhood sexual abuse, domestic violence, sexual exploitation, or who committed sexually abusive acts.
- There is no single approach that works best for every individual.
- Interventions that work best are multifaceted, tailored to assessed psychosocial needs, intensive and, usually, long term.
- It is most helpful to think in terms of a "toolkit" of approaches, each of which may be useful at a particular stage for a particular individual. [Department of Health, in preparation]

The Government committed to improving access to psychological therapies in its 2005 manifesto, and the *Improving Access to Psychological Therapies* programme (IAPT) was launched in May 2006. The programme forms part of the delivery of the *Our Health, Our Care, Our Say* White Paper. It aims to provide better access to a choice of evidence-based psychological therapies for people suffering from depression and anxiety disorders (Department of Health, 2007).

IAPT is concerned with raising standards of recognition and treatment for the many people who suffer from depression and anxiety disorders. The programme is at the heart of the government's drive to give greater access to, and choice of, talking therapies to those who would benefit from them.

However, even in the short term, the success rate for cognitive–behavioural therapy in people with depression and anxiety is only 50% (Centre for Economic Performance's Mental Health Policy Group, 2006). Many of the people who do not respond will do so because they have more complex needs. Psychotherapeutic interventions for people with more complex needs represent an important component of the delivery of National Health Service (NHS) mental health services. However, they fall outside of the scope of the IAPT programme. One of the aims of the new IAPT services is to reduce the burden on specialist services, allowing them to better meet the needs of people with more complex problems.

Some people with more complex needs may be treated through specialist personality disorder services using the evidence based treatments as provided in centres of excellence such as the Halliwick Day Hospital and the Cassel Hospital, among others (National Institute for Mental Health in England (NIMHE), 2003). Most will be treated in local specialist psychotherapy services in Community Mental Health Teams and in other specialist psychotherapy services. Many will be treated in the independent and voluntary sectors.

Children and adolescents

Every Child Matters: Change for Children (HM Government, 2004) sets the national framework for access to a wide range of locally provided specialist services, and emphasizes the importance of targeted specialist services for children and young people. *Think Family* (Cabinet Office Social Exclusion Task Force, 2006b, 2008) describes a new approach to improve support for the most disadvantaged families and to prevent problems being passed down from excluded parents to their children through tackling the root causes of children's difficulties through tailored support rather than one-size-fits-all services.

Key messages

1. Sexual abuse, violence, and neglect in childhood may affect essential aspects of a child or adolescent's emotional development and the development of their brain. The impact of abuse

on children and adolescents is complex, involving degrees of sexual, physical, and emotional abuse, and neglect. Different types of abuse and neglect occur together. Disorganized attachment and dissociative symptoms are important harmful effects of child abuse and neglect.

2. The impact of child abuse on an individual's development can persist through the life-cycle and may be more evident at times of change, e.g., puberty, adolescence, parenthood, bereavement. Therapeutic help should be available when needed.

3. Psychoanalytic psychotherapy and other psychoanalytically based treatments have been shown to be effective in the treatment of the emotional consequences of child abuse. The focus on attachment and attachment difficulties in the therapeutic relationship is particularly important for people who have attachment difficulties that are commonly associated with childhood abuse and neglect.

4. The type, timing, duration, and intensity of psychotherapy will depend on the individual and their wishes, their history, and the family and social context.

5. Sexual abuse, violence, and neglect occur frequently to children. However, non-disclosure is the norm. Even after disclosure, the extent of the problem might not be recognized or properly assessed, and individuals and families might not get the help that they need.

6. People who have experienced childhood sexual abuse, violence, or neglect might have persisting dissociative symptoms and show disorganized attachment. The proper assessment of these individuals is complex and might require several sessions before appropriate treatment recommendations can safely be made.

7. Stepped care requires high quality assessment to be effective and avoid offering inappropriate treatments that may at best waste patients' time and service resources, and at worst be harmful. This is may occur when offering treatments to people with complex dissociative problems and disorganized attachment.

8. Assessment and treatment of people who have been abused as children is complex and emotionally disturbing. Staff themselves may experience secondary traumatization from repeated

exposure to their patients' experiences of abuse. Staff working
in this area should have access to regular supervision or consultation with an adult psychotherapist or consultant psychiatrist
in psychotherapy, or child and adolescent psychotherapist,
depending on the patient group.

9. Child abuse by women is under-recognized and its seriousness
and effects often minimized. Female abusers are less likely to be
assessed or treated appropriately.

10. The independent and voluntary sectors play a significant role
in providing psychotherapy resources to people who have
experienced childhood abuse and neglect.

Children and adolescents

1. Ideally, qualified child and adolescent psychotherapists would
carry out assessments of children and adolescents who have
been abused. However, where there are insufficient numbers of
qualified child and adolescent psychotherapists, there is a need
for regular supervision by qualified child and adolescent
psychotherapists.

2. Child abuse usually arises within the family and will affect the
whole family. Parents and carers of abused children need ongoing help to understand the impact of the abuse on the child's
behaviour and on the family. Family therapy, where appropriate, can help children, adolescent patients, and their families
through periods of crisis and to understand how the abuse
arose.

3. Sibling abuse needs to be understood as a problem requiring
expert therapeutic help for both victim and perpetrator, and for
the parents to understand why this occurred within the family
and what changes are needed to ensure the future safety of the
children.

Recommendations

1. People who have been subjected to childhood sexual abuse,
violence, or neglect should have access to effective psychotherapies. This should include psychoanalytic psychotherapy.

2. Long-term individual psychotherapeutic treatment needs to be available to those who require it to work through the complex emotional consequences and attachment difficulties caused by child abuse. Psychoanalytic psychotherapy is important because of its focus on attachment and attachment difficulties in the therapeutic relationship.

3. Group and family work should be available, when appropriate, and can be combined effectively with long-term individual psychotherapeutic work.

4. Stepped care services should pilot or implement stepped assessments to identify people with histories of childhood sexual abuse, violence, neglect, or dissociative symptoms at early stages of stepped care programmes, in order to avoid offering inappropriate, wasteful, or harmful treatments.

5. Pilot projects are needed that can incorporate and evaluate psychoanalytically based treatments for people who have experienced childhood sexual abuse, violence, or neglect.

6. Staff working with people who have experienced childhood sexual abuse, violence, or neglect should have access to regular supervision or consultation with an adult psychotherapist or consultant psychiatrist in psychotherapy, or child and adolescent psychotherapist, as they are at risk of secondary traumatization from repeated exposure to their patients' experiences of abuse.

7. The voluntary and independent sectors have a wealth of expertise and should be involved in specialist training and supervision.

Children and adolescents

1. Expert psychotherapeutic assessment and treatment is needed for children and adolescents who have experienced abuse and neglect. Ideally, qualified child and adolescent psychotherapists would carry out this. However, where there are insufficient numbers of qualified child and adolescent psychotherapists, there is a need for regular supervision by qualified child and adolescent psychotherapists.

2. Parents and carers of abused children should receive help to understand the impact of the abuse on the child's behaviour and on the family, and to understand how the abuse arose.

3. Sibling abuse requires expert psychotherapeutic help for both victim and perpetrator, and for the parents to understand why the abuse occurred within the family and what changes are needed to ensure the future safety of the children.

Background

Child abuse, whether it is sexual, physical, or emotional abuse, or neglect, are experiences, not clinical conditions. Different types of abuse co-exist (Ney, Fung, & Wickett, 1994). Neither does child abuse exist in a vacuum. Abused children often have to contend with a host of other difficulties as well; child disability or ill health, parenting problems, parental history of being a child victim of abuse, parental mental ill health or emotional impairment, parental substance misuse, domestic violence, poverty. This wide range of child, family, and parental adverse circumstances all interact and influence each other. The consequences of child abuse and child sexual abuse are equally protean, and appear to be influenced by the environment and the availability of good experiences with other parents or carers (Jones & Ramchandani, 1999).

Extent of the problem

- 20–30% of girls are sexually abused.
- 10–15% of boys are sexually abused.

- Sexual abuse of children is associated with other forms of abuse, neglect, and adversity.
- Combinations of different types of abuse are most harmful.

Fortunately, there is now widespread professional recognition of the reality that children are regularly abused, sexually, physically, and emotionally. However, in individual cases it is still not unusual for signs to be missed, and allegations to be dismissed, or victims to be pressured to withdraw their allegations; sadly, often from within the family.

Prevalence rates for child sexual abuse and domestic violence are high, although the precise figures are dependent on the definitions of abuse used.

Sexual abuse may be classified as non-contact or contact, with contact sexual abuse divided into penetrative and non-penetrative forms. Extreme forms of ritualized or sadistic abuse occur.

Non-contact sexual abuse includes inappropriate exposure, of victim or perpetrator, or exposure to pornography. Non-penetrative contact abuse includes touching, kissing, masturbation. Penetrative abuse includes oral, vaginal, and anal penetration. Child sexual abuse may range from a single episode to decades of abuse.

There are many large studies that have consistently shown rates of all types of sexual abuse of 20–30% for girls and 10–15% for boys; these figures have been replicated across continents, countries, social classes, and ethnic groups, showing little variation (Baker & Duncan, 1985; Finkelhor, 1994a; Itzin, 2000; Kelly, Regan, & Burton, 1991; Mama, 2000; Mrazek, Lynch, & Bentovim, 1983; Patel, 2000).

A meta-analysis of studies of non-clinical samples found that the relative frequencies of different types of abuse were: exhibitionism 33% (females 38%, males 25%) fondling 68% (females 67%, males 69%) oral sex 14% (females 9%, males 22%) sexual intercourse 15% (females 16%, males 13%) (Rind, Tromovitch, & Bauserman, 1998).

> Mrs A was first raped by her father aged four. Then until her late teens she was regularly sexually abused by a group of her parents' friends including men and women. She managed not to think about her experience of abuse, until a sexual assault as an adult led to overwhelming memories. She received little benefit from outpatient treatment. She eventually sought treatment in a residential psychotherapeutic hospital. [Case history, McQueen]

There is a substantial body of knowledge about the nature, extent, and effects of child sexual and physical abuse, domestic violence, rape and sexual assault, and sexual exploitation as it affects victims, survivors, and abusers, including children, adolescents, and adults, both male and female (Hanmer & Itzin, 2000; Itzin, 2000).

Government statistics for England show that during the twelve months to the end of March 2007, there were 33,300 children who became subject of a child protection plan. There were 27,900 children in England who were the subject of a plan at 31 March 2007. This is twenty-five children per 10,000 of the population aged under eighteen. Seventy-eight per cent of children who were the subject of a Local Authority child protection plan were in foster placements and 12% were placed with their own parents.

Neglect was the most common category of abuse (14,800 children, 44%), followed by emotional abuse (7,800 children, 23%), physical abuse (5,100 children, 15%), then sexual abuse (2,500, 7%) (Department for Children, Schools and Families, 2007). Clearly, only a tiny proportion of all the children who are exposed to abuse in the home become subject to a Local Authority child protection plan.

The context of abuse

Associated with child sexual abuse are high rates of physical abuse of children, exposure to domestic violence, and verbal abuse (Cawson, Wattam, Brooker, & Kelly, 2000). There is evidence of co-occurrence of domestic violence with child sexual abuse and physical abuse, also of sexual assault with domestic violence (Mullender & Morley, 1994; Walby & Allen, 2004). There is evidence of the effects of domestic violence on the mental and physical health of children and women (Hanmer & Itzin, 2000; Humphreys & Thiara, 2003). The effects of exposure to different types of abuse are additive (Ney, Fung, & Wickett, 1994).

It can be difficult to disentangle the effects of different types of child abuse or neglect from other adverse childhood experiences such as witnessing domestic violence, poor parenting, parental substance misuse, parental mental health problems, social exclusion, or poverty.

As these difficulties tend to occur together it is difficult to know which of the different types of abuse or parental, family, social, economic, or other factors are causing the poorer outcomes for the children. Therefore, when conducting research in this area, it is important that researchers take into account, and control for, the different types of adversity to which these children are exposed.

Unfortunately, many studies in this area do not control for other types of adversity. One systematic review of the effects on children of witnessing domestic violence found that fewer than 20% of the studies controlled for social class and none of the studies controlled for parental substance misuse (Kitzmann, Gaylord, Holt, & Kenny, 2003). It is possible that parental substance misuse could account for much, or even all, of the worse outcomes shown by the children in these families, and social class may also contribute significantly.

One series of studies involving a community sample of women controlled for other childhood adversity. It demonstrated that childhood sexual abuse was associated with adult psychiatric disorder, low self-esteem, deliberate self-harm, eating disorders, sexual problems, teenage pregnancy, relationship difficulties, and increased divorce rates. However, childhood sexual abuse on its own was neither necessary nor sufficient to produce these problems, as other childhood risk factors, such as poor parental mental health, poor relationships with parents, or physical abuse also contributed to negative adult outcomes. The authors concluded that childhood sexual abuse acts in concert with a range of other adverse factors in producing adverse outcomes (Mullen, Roman-Clarkson, & Walton, 1988).

A meta-analysis of fifty-nine retrospective studies of child sexual abuse reported by college students found that child sexual abuse had a small effect size on psychological adjustment. Furthermore, that family environment factors explained nine times more of the variation in emotional symptoms than did child sexual abuse (Rind, Tromovitch, & Bauserman, 1998). It is important to note that this meta-analysis only looked at college students, a selected group of individuals who are functioning at an above-average level. Had the meta-analysis included clinical samples, it would have included individuals who had been more severely affected, and it is likely that the results would have been different.

Children exposed to domestic violence alone show emotional and behavioural problems, social and educational failure, and drug misuse (Hester, Pearson, & Harwin, 2000).

> A therapist in a specialist unit uses play therapy equipment to allow each child to explore their own world, the worker listens and gently draws them out through the play activities. One seven-year-old girl who was helped in this way just sat and played with sand for the first eight weeks until she felt ready to progress. She was the youngest in the family and had been demonstrating quite aggressive behaviour. Her advocacy worker felt she would benefit from some space for herself while the family was on the waiting list for parenting work. This child showed real improvements, becoming able to sleep and use the toilet on her own, which previously she had been too frightened to do, and generally feeling more confident. In addition, children and families were referred to several other agencies, including social services for child protection issues and the local Family Service Unit for family work. [Mullender, 2004, p. 33]

A study of 167 children and adolescents in a mixed sample including young psychiatric patients, young offenders, and non-symptomatic high school children considered combinations of different types of abuse (sexual abuse, physical abuse, physical neglect, verbal abuse, emotional neglect). The study found that the combination of physical abuse, physical neglect, and verbal abuse correlated most strongly with adjustment problems. In the ten worst combinations, verbal abuse appeared seven times, physical neglect six times, physical abuse and emotional neglect five times each, and child sexual abuse occurred only once (Ney, Fung, & Wickett, 1994).

Other studies have also demonstrated that emotional abuse in the form of verbal abuse is a particularly damaging form of child abuse leading to an increased risk of personality disorder, even after controlling for other forms of abuse and adversity (Johnson et al., 2001). The combination of verbal abuse and witnessing domestic violence may be associated with the greatest adverse effects, particularly dissociation (Teicher, Samson, Polcari, & McGreenery, 2006).

These studies, taken together, show that different types of abuse occur together. It is rather artificial to focus on one type of abuse and ignore the others. The combination of different types of abuse and neglect appears most damaging to children's development. Sexual abuse, physical abuse, emotional abuse, and neglect all cover a spectrum of severity and duration, and individuals have different vulnerabilities and resilience. Averaging these abuses out across groups for the purposes of statistical presentation or ranking obscures the nature of the individual's experience and the meaning that it has for them.

The accumulated wisdom of years of in-depth psychotherapeutic work and work by doctors, nurses, teachers, social workers, and others with people who have experienced early trauma shows that sexual, physical, and emotional abuse or neglect in childhood can have profoundly disruptive effects on the development of the mind and that it is understanding the uniqueness of the individual's experiences, the feelings and meanings attached to those experiences, that provide the therapeutic key to ameliorating the after effects of abuse.

Symptoms and effects in childhood

It has been argued that child sexual abuse, violence, and neglect covers an enormous range of acts and omissions that take place in widely differing family settings, with widely varying family and community resources on which the child might or might not be able to draw. And it might happen to children at different ages, over different periods of time, and these children might individually have widely varying strengths or vulnerabilities.

Children can respond to these very different experiences with a wide range of symptoms and levels of emotional disturbance. Although these patterns vary to some extent with age, there is no fixed general sexual abuse syndrome.

Not all children will develop obvious symptoms; some studies have shown that up to 40% of children will show few symptoms if assessed by standard instruments (Kendall-Tackett, Williams, & Finkelhor, 1993). Some of the children in this group might be without obvious symptoms because they are dealing with the abuse successfully; they might be particularly resilient and have parents or attachment figures who have helped them cope.

Unfortunately, this group also contains children with an avoidant coping style, who have managed the abuse by avoiding thinking about it, by compartmentalizing it in their mind; this may be a successful strategy in the short term, but may lead to longer term difficulties (Finkelhor & Berliner, 1995; Kennedy, 1996). Dissociation normally reduces through early childhood as children develop an integrated sense of self. However, this process of integration is inhibited in children who have been maltreated; they tend to show *increasing* levels of dissociation as time passes (MacFie, Cicchetti, & Toth, 2001). Dissociation and failure to achieve an integrated sense of self inhibits the ability to think about the mental states of oneself and others in a coherent way; this is known as reflective function. Reflective function is inhibited by maltreatment in childhood (Fonagy, Gergely, Jurist, & Target, 2004).

These children who are apparently without symptoms, but are relying heavily on dissociation to avoid integrating their abusive experiences, might have most to gain from a proper in-depth psychodynamic assessment if it can lead to appropriate psychotherapeutic treatment.

The experience of sexual abuse in childhood can, for some children, lead to a range of emotional, academic, social, and behavioural problems in childhood. These include increased rates of academic difficulties, post traumatic stress disorder, conduct disorder, and, for a minority, sexualized behaviour (Kendall-Tackett, Williams, & Finkelhor, 1993; Spataro, Mullen, Burgess, Wells, & Moss, 2004), promiscuity, and suicidal thoughts and behaviour (Paolucci, Genuis, & Violato, 2001).

A small number of children, usually those who have been exposed to multiple forms of abuse, particularly witnessing domestic violence, physical abuse, and neglect are at increased risk of engaging in sexually harmful behaviour in childhood and adolescence (Hickey, Vizard, McCrory, & French, 2006; Skuse et al., 1998). However, most of these will not continue to commit sexual offences against children in adulthood (Bentovim & Williams, 1998).

Later symptoms and effects

Child sexual abuse in earlier life has multiple effects and interactions affecting later development across the life span, affecting future mental health, physical health, sexual relationships, and parenting.

High rates of child abuse and sexual abuse are reported by adults with many psychiatric conditions (Bulik, Prescott, & Kendler, 2001; Greenfield et al., 1994; MacMillan et al., 2001; Spataro, Mullen, Burgess, Wells, & Moss, 2004; Vize & Cooper, 1995); personality disorders (especially borderline personality disorder and dissocial [antisocial] personality disorder); post traumatic stress disorder; dissociative disorders (multiple personality disorder, dissociative identity disorder, depersonalization) (Sinason, 2002a), depression (Bifulco, Brown, & Adler, 1991), anxiety disorders (generalized anxiety disorder and panic disorder) eating disorders, and psychosis. There is also inconclusive evidence of a link with schizophrenia (Morgan & Fisher, 2007). The World Health Organization found that, internationally, child sexual abuse contributed between 4% and 5% of the burden of disease in males and between 7% and 8% of the burden of disease in females, for depression, alcohol dependency, and drug misuse. The attributable fractions were higher for panic disorder (7% for males and 13% for females) and higher still for PTSD (21% for males and 33% for females). For suicide attempts, attributable fractions were 6% for males and 11% for females (Andrews, Corry, Slade, Issakidis, & Swanston, 2004).

There is a relationship between the type of the abuse and the severity of psychiatric disturbance. One study found that adults who had experienced penetrative sexual abuse as children were sixteen times more likely to be admitted to psychiatric hospital (Read, 1998).

In children and adolescents, a spectrum of dissociative symptoms are associated with sexual and physical abuse (Coons, 1996; Dell & Eisenhower, 1990; Hornstein & Putnam, 1992; MacFie, Cicchetti, & Toth, 2001; Trickett, Noll, Reiffman, & Putnam, 2001) and with parental neglect (Brunner, Parzer, Schuld, & Resch, 2000; Ogawa, Sroufe, Weinfield, Carlson, & Egeland, 1997; Sanders & Giolas, 1991). Ninety per cent of people with Dissociative Identity Disorder—a severe form of dissociative disorder - have been found to have a history of childhood sexual abuse (Fonagy & Target, 1995). People with dissociative disorders are at particularly high risk of repeated suicide attempts (Foote, Smolin, Neft, & Lipschitz, 2008).

Adults with psychosomatic conditions report elevated and vastly elevated rates of childhood sexual abuse; adults with other physical conditions not generally regarded as psychosomatic (irritable bowel syndrome, chronic fatigue syndrome, fibromyalgia, chronic pelvic pain, chronic bladder problems, chronic headache including migraine, asthma, diabetes, and heart problems) also report elevated rates of childhood sexual abuse (Arnold, Rogers, & Cook, 1990; Leserman, 2005; Romans, Belaise, Martin, Morris, & Raffi, 2002). Additionally, experiencing child sexual abuse is associated with other health risk behaviours: for example, smoking, substance misuse, and obesity, which contribute to the excess long-term health problems (Felitti et al., 1998; Noll, Zeller, Trickett, & Putnam, 2007).

Adolescents and adults who have experienced childhood sexual abuse are more likely to engage in risky sexual behaviour (Brown, Craig, Harris, & Handley, 2008). There is more promiscuity and more sexually transmitted infection (Felitti et al., 1998). Other studies have found that sexually abused girls become sexually active at an earlier age, practice less effective contraception and have higher rates of teen motherhood (Noll, Trickett, & Putnam, 2003b). One prospective study of children whose childhood sexual abuse had been proven in court found that these children went on to be 27.7 times more likely to be arrested for prostitution than matched controls that had not been sexually abused (C. S. Widom, 1989).

Research at the Cassel Hospital has indicated that adults who have had abusive experiences in childhood, and who develop limited reflective function, are less likely to resolve their abuse, and are also more likely to manifest borderline pathology (Fonagy et al., 1996). If the abused child or adult has access to a relationship that can help them deal with the emotional impact of their abuse, they can, to some degree, resolve the experience; they might then be protected from severe borderline pathology (Healy & Kennedy, 1993).

People who have experienced sexual, physical, or emotional abuse are more likely to have difficulties in intimate relationships, and describe their own adult relationships as less rewarding, less stable, or more violent and abusive (Mullen, Martin, Anderson, Romans, & Herbison, 1996). Sexually abused boys and girls have increased rates of self-harm in adolescence and increased revictimization in adolescence and adulthood (Hawton, Rodham, Evans, & Weatherall, 2002; Kendall-Tackett, Williams, & Finkelhor, 1993).

There is evidence of intergenerational effects of violence and abuse. Children who are maltreated as children are more likely as adults to maltreat their own children. A prospective study of parenting and children found that parents who had been sexually abused as children were more likely to treat their children in a way that amounted to maltreatment: 40% of maltreated parents were independently observed to maltreat their children, 30% provided borderline care (suspected maltreatment) and 30% provided clearly adequate care. Almost all of the parents who had a history of loving care in their childhood provided adequate care for their children (Egeland, Jacobvitz, & Papatola, 1987; Egeland, Jacobvitz, & Sroufe, 1988; Sroufe, Egeland, Carlson, & Collins, 2005; University of Minnesota).

In the Minnesota study, it was found that the parents who had experienced maltreatment in their childhoods but did not go on to maltreat their own children were characterized by three features. Abused mothers who provided adequate care to their children were significantly more likely to have received emotional support from an alternative, non-abusive adult during childhood, and/or, second, to have participated in therapy of at least six months duration at some point in their lives. These two factors each applied to about 50% of the mothers who broke the cycle of abuse, but almost none of those abused mothers who went on to maltreat their children. Furthermore, almost all of the mothers who broke the cycle of abuse had a satisfying partner relationship as an adult. The authors point out that each of these change-promoting factors is a relationship experience (Sroufe, Egeland, Carlson, & Collins, 2005).

A review of the literature on the intergenerational transmission of child abuse concluded that one third of those who are abused as children grow up to continue a pattern of inept or abusive parenting, one third do not, and one third remain vulnerable to social stress and to becoming abusive parents (Oliver, 1993). The single most important modifying factor in the generational transmission of child abuse was found to be if the child victim was able to grow up with the ability to face the emotional reality of their past and present personal relationships.

There is a link for some boys between having been sexually abused as a child and subsequently perpetrating sexual abuse as adolescents and adults (C. P. Widom, 1989). Historically, adult sexual offenders have reported high rates of having been abused as children themselves. However, recent studies suggest that when convicted child sexual offenders are assessed by polygraph (lie detector), the number claiming a history of sexual victimization in their own childhood falls from 60% to 30% (Hindman & Peters, 2001).

Department of Health funded research has identified the additional roles of physical abuse and witnessing domestic violence, together with child sexual abuse, in creating vulnerability for sexual offending against children (Skuse et al., 1998).

The children of people who have been sexually abused are at greater risk of being abused themselves. In a study of children referred to NCH specialist child sexual abuse projects, almost two-thirds of the children's carers had experienced sexual or physical violence as a child or adult themselves (NCH, 2004).

Sometimes, the effects of child abuse remain largely hidden, only to emerge at key times in later life, e.g., puberty, adolescence as people start to explore intimate love relationships, pregnancy, motherhood, and fatherhood. Or later abusive experiences may reopen old wounds. Furthermore, women who have experienced childhood sexual abuse report twice as many subsequent sexual assaults as those without a history of abuse (Noll, Horowitz, Bonnano, Trickett, & Putnam, 2003a).

Memories of child abuse

Research on memory has shown that:

- Very early abuse, before the age of two, does not appear to be recorded as memories of events, in the normal autobiographical sense, due to the immaturity of the brain memory systems.
- Abuse that occurs after the age of four may be, to some extent, remembered as events.
- Abuse that occurs between the ages of two and four may be remembered in some form, but is distorted.
- Abuse may be forgotten: the commonest way for this to occur is through dissociation,

- Abuse at any age leads to a distortion of the mind and of relationships that may lead the survivor to get into repetitive patterns of behaviour and relating that can suggest a history of abuse. There can also be problems with learning and thinking that may be revealed in some types of learning difficulty.

Occasionally, people rediscover or recover memories of being abused as children during psychotherapy, so called "recovered memories". The area of recovered memories has generated a great deal of controversy and distress for individuals and families. It would appear that in some cases the recovered memories might have a historical basis and can be corroborated or confirmed. In other cases, historical abuse remains a possibility; in some cases dubious therapeutic techniques and suggestions made by the therapist may have stimulated the construction of a false memory (Target, 1998). For a description of a case of memory loss and recovered memory after authenticated incestuous sexual abuse, see Duggal and Sroufe (1998) (also reported in Sroufe, Egeland, Carlson, & Collins, 2005, pp. 269–270).

The psychotherapist needs to be wary of unconscious coercion on their part, either to suggest abusing memories or to help to deny them (Kennedy, 1996).

Recovered memories of abuse

A woman in analysis got into a difficult work relationship. She would constantly complain about a man at work who was mistreating her and abusing her. This was someone on whom she had pinned great hopes, and his treatment of her was a great disappointment to her. Initially the psychoanalyst thought that this material referred to himself, however interpreting the material in this way made little difference to her sense of being misused. There were indications of some parental failure; the parents had tended to leave her and her sibling in the care of relatives from time to time. The fact that she was left in my care in the analysis, that she felt abused at work, that she had a certain amount of difficulty in dealing with fantasy and dreams, that she was also rather controlling of her psychoanalyst in the sessions, and that there had been significant gaps in her parenting, made the analyst suspect some kind of childhood abuse.

Eventually he wondered with her if she had actually been molested in some way as a child. The question produced some relief, and, soon after, memories of sexual abuse by an uncle, which she had kept to herself as a child and then forgotten. Her sense of grievance towards the work-figure retreated. She never wanted to seek revenge, either on her uncle or her parents, for what had happened. Nor did the abuse become the major focus of the analysis. In this instance and after careful consideration the psychoanalyst felt that the abuse had actually occurred. [Adapted from Kennedy, 1996]

During the course of a successful psychotherapy, the patient will necessarily undergo shifts in their perception of the nature of the abuse. What is likely to be most helpful to the patient is neither a "for" nor an "against" position in relation to the accounts of the abuse, but an "alongside" the patient as they discover how the abuse has affected their mind and their relationships.

Neutrality is not disbelief. But neither is it belief and, because it is not it closes off avenues of discovery gated by entrances which need the key of belief. When I ask, "Do you believe me?" I am not asking, "Do you know for certain this really happened to me?" I know you weren't there so you cannot know that what I recall in fragments is objectively true memory of exactly what was done to me. And that is not what I am seeking with my question. What I need is reassurance that you trust me; that you believe I am not lying; that you believe that what I tell you is my truth; that my recollections of extreme cruelty are not beyond the realms of belief. To walk beside me you must believe human beings are capable of inflicting the kind of abuse and horror that I remember. Demonstrating you do is the key of belief you can give without compromising therapeutic neutrality. [IS, 2006]

Child abuse linked to spiritual or religious belief

Seemingly nowhere is the pressure to believe or disbelieve so great as in the area of organized child abuse by paedophile networks or rings, and where abusers invoke religious or supernatural forces in the abuse. This pressure to believe or disbelieve may be related to the states of mindless terror that occur to children abused in these ways. The polarization of opinion into for and against is likely to be unhelpful to the people who have had such experiences and to those who try to help them.

The National Society for the Prevention of Cruelty to Children has published guidance highlighting how personal, religious, organizational, and social factors can inhibit safeguarding children in religious matters and organizations (Edwards, 2005[2007]).

The Department for Education and Skills has commissioned research on child abuse linked to accusations of possession and witchcraft, and published guidance on child abuse linked to a belief in spirit possession (Stobart, 2006; Department for Education and Skills, 2007). These documents emphasize that, while numbers of such cases of child abuse are small compared to the total number of abused children, the impact on the child is great, causing substantial and serious harm to the abused children. It is commented that victims who become convinced that they are possessed might require years of support.

It is also noted that significantly larger numbers of cases might remain undetected and might come to light as this type of abuse is openly discussed and awareness is raised.

Both documents describe the extreme and serious abuse that may occur: physical abuse (beating, shaking, stabbing, cutting, burning, tying up, strangulation, suffocation, cold baths, holding under water, rubbing chilli and other substances into children's eyes, genitals and mouths, breaking bones and killing); emotional abuse (ignoring and isolating the child, telling them that they are evil or possessed, which the child may come to believe, threats of abandonment); neglect (fasting and starvation, exposure to cold, forced sleeping in baths, failure to ensure medical treatment or attendance at school); sexual abuse: it is noted that children abused in these ways may be particularly vulnerable to sexual exploitation, perhaps because they feel particularly powerless, worthless and feel that they will not be believed if they tell someone about the abuse.

In over a quarter of the cases in the DfES research there were concerns about the mental health of the carer, specifically post traumatic stress disorder, depression, and schizophrenia.

At risk children

Some groups of children and adults are at more risk of sexual or physical abuse or neglect than others, particularly:

- disabled children;
- children with chronic illnesses;
- deaf children;
- socially excluded families;
- previously abused children;
- children in the care system;
- refugees and asylum seekers;
- trafficked children.

Children with disabilities

> It is very difficult to teach and learn about the survival of trauma by those with learning disabilities, especially the young, because when we take on board the scope of the problem and the magnitude of the despair and desperation associated with it, we all experience extreme anxiety . . .
>
> We are reminded of the strength and prevalence of denial concerning the suffering of children who are abused, which, in the case of those with learning disabilities, is even more extreme. [Hopper, 2002]

- Children and adults with disabilities are at increased risk of sexual abuse.
- Children and adults with disabilities experience more physical abuse.
- Children and adults with disabilities experience more neglect.
- Trauma and neglect cause learning disability.
- Sexual abuse of people with disabilities is less likely to be detected or reported.
- People with disabilities receive least sex education.

People with learning disabilities are at greatly increased risk of sexual abuse (Westcott, 1991). The risk of abuse and sexual abuse may be as much as three times higher (Sobsey, Grey, Wells, Pyper, & Reimer-Heck, 1991; Sullivan & Scanlan, 1988). As many as 90% of people with developmental disabilities will experience some form of sexual abuse at some point in their lives (Valenti-Hein & Schwartz, 1995). Thirty-nine–sixty-eight per cent of learning disabled girls and 16–30% of learning disabled boys will be sexually abused before their eighteenth birthday (Sobsey, 1994). In a sample of adults with learning disabilities, 61% of the women and 25% of the men had been sexually abused (McCarthy & Thompson, 1992). Among people with learning disability attending a day centre in America, 83% of the women and 32% of the men reported sexual abuse (Hard & Plumb, 1987).

Physical disability leads to an increased risk for abuse (Ammerman, Van Hasselt, & Hersen, 1988b; Caplan & Dinardo, 1986; Garbarino, 1987; Starr, Dietrich, Fischoff, Ceresnie, & Zweier, 1984; Zirpoli, 1990). Sixty-nine per cent of hospital admissions of children and adolescents with multiple handicaps were due to physical abuse in one study (Ammerman, Van Hasselt, Hersen, McGonigle, & Lubetsky, 1989).

Deaf children appear to be especially at risk of abuse. In America, 54% of boys and 50% of girls with hearing impairment report abuse (Kennedy, 1990). Individual residential schools for deaf children have also reported incidences of abuse of 50% (Sullivan, Vernon, & Scanlan, 1987). In Norway, deaf females reported experiencing child sexual abuse with contact more than twice as often as hearing females, and deaf males more than three times as often as hearing males. The abuse of the deaf children was also more serious, and few cases were reported to parents, teachers, or authorities (Kvam, 2004).

Brain damage itself can be the result of physical abuse: studies have found that 3–13% of cerebral palsy and learning disability is due to physical violence (Buchanan & Oliver, 1979; Diamond & Jaudes, 1983; Oliver, 1988; Sternfeld, 1977).

The majority of mild learning disability in the UK is thought to be acquired due to environmental adversity, such as lowest social class, poverty, large number of siblings, paternal unemployment, and maternal deprivation (Reiser & Mason, 1990; Ricks, 1990; Rutter, Tizard, & Whitmore, 1970).

Historical studies have demonstrated that extreme emotional neglect in institutions for infants causes severe developmental delay and even increased mortality from infections, despite good hygiene and physical care (Spitz, 1945).

While it is largely understood that children and adults with a learning disability are sexual beings and expressing sexuality is a normal and instinctual developmental task, the reality falls far short. People with learning disabilities are able to use adapted sex education (Haseltine & Miltenberger, 1990).

Sex education leads to lower rates of sexual abuse. However, the sexuality of people with a learning disability is something that is frequently ignored (Craft & Craft, 1981; Elwood, 1981).

Psychodynamic psychotherapy with people with learning disabilities

Historically, learning disability has been considered an exclusion criterion for talking therapies generally and psychodynamic psychotherapy in particular. Learning disability is still often used as an exclusion criterion in research into psychological therapies, and consequently there are few rigorous outcome studies of psychotherapies on this group (Sinason, 2002b).

However there is now increased recognition of the importance of emotional meaning in the lives of people with learning disability and an increased awareness of their heightened vulnerability to sexual abuse and multiple experiences of loss (Royal College of Psychiatrists, 2004; Sequiera & Hollins, 2003).

> 27-year-old Ms C kept wheeling her wheelchair into the furthest part of the room and banging her head against the wall. Staff had tried fitting her with a helmet and padding the wall, but to no avail. Ms C was offered psychotherapy; in treatment the link was made with the bad thoughts and memories of sexual abuse in her head that she wished that she could bang out of existence. The head banging stopped. [Sinason, 2002b, p. 428]

A large number of publications by the Royal College of Psychiatrists, including a Joint Report with the British Psychological Society and reports from the Department of Health, stress that psychological therapy services are a vital component of effective mental health care, that services should be inclusive, and there should be equality of access to mainstream services, including specialist mental health and psychotherapies (Royal College of Psychiatrists, 1997, 2004; Royal College of Psychiatrists & British Psychological Society, 1995; Department of Health, 2000, 2001a, 2001b.

There are many examples of current services for people with learning disabilities, ranging from highly-specialized services, providing individual and group psychoanalytic therapy, through to individuals or groups of clinicians within services that work at the level of facilitating psychotherapeutic understanding in the day-to-day work of carers, professionals, and support staff. Traditional psychodynamic therapies have developed, and now the psychotherapeutic models most written about with regard to people with learning disabilities are psychodynamic (Royal College of Psychiatrists, 2004).

People with learning disabilities may be rather passive and find it difficult to express negative feelings towards people on whom they depend. The verbalization of these feelings is central in the psychodynamic treatment of people who have adopted an "appeasement" posture of smiling, pseudo-compliance to defend against the trauma of being different or fears of the therapist's hatred of them (Sinason, 1992).

> Charles walked up and down the corridor all day, looking desperately left and right and then behind him. Psychotherapy, informed by trauma knowledge, revealed that this was hypervigilance. Charles' father who had psychotic episodes used to burst in and attack him. When the therapist was able to explore Charles' fear that someone else could attack him, he was able to reduce this behaviour. Until the reason for the behaviour could be explored staff felt unable to offer support, they had thought that this was either obsessive or autistic behaviour or ADHD. [Sinason, 2002b, p. 427]

A number of authors have described group analytic work with people with learning disabilities, and where there has been a persistence of this approach, lasting benefits have been observed. Just as with individual work, adaptations to the traditional functioning of group therapies might need to be made and account taken of particular contextual issues, such as mode of referral, how voluntary an individual's presence might or might not be, the expectations of carers and other professionals, transport, and communication with others about individual or group issues. Group work can have a specific focus, such as sexual offending or bereavement, and may use varied techniques, including pictures, stories, and mime (MacDonald, Sinason, & Hollins, 2003).

People with learning disabilities may have considerable difficulties in both independent and supported travel. Without support for travel, psychotherapy may be ruled out or fail, regardless of their ability to make use of it. Some people can become more independent during a period of treatment, but others will always need regular support. This is not an easy or straightforward task for care workers or, indeed, for families to undertake. Staffing shortages and inconsistencies and financial restraints can impede regular attendance at sessions. Attendance for therapy may give rise to complex feelings in the carers, such as envy or impatience with the time taken. Those escorting the patient may be curious about what they are doing with the therapist and find it difficult not to question them. Paid carers may well have their own difficulties that drew them into this field, and it can be painful to see those they care for receiving the professional help that they might wish for themselves. This may lead to the therapy being undermined, and emphasizes the need to address the whole process and support system around the patient (Royal College of Psychiatrists, 2004).

> Andrew was being assaulted by another patient at his day centre; he had not been able to discuss this with his worker because he felt ashamed. It reminded him of the physical abuse that he received as a child from his father and a schoolteacher. He was referred for therapy only when his behaviour deteriorated.

> His therapist wrote a letter on his behalf: "I am writing in the presence of Andrew, at his request and with his permission. He is very sad and frightened at the moment because he is being bullied at his day centre and that is why he has been behaving in a disturbed way." [Sinason, 2002b, p. 427]

Socially excluded children

By definition, socially excluded children are over-represented in multiple categories of disadvantage, and have least access to appropriate services. The government has acknowledged the huge burden of disadvantage and its intergenerational transmission, the cycle of disadvantage and deprivation. There is recognition that the problems of the most excluded are multi-faceted (Cabinet Office Social Exclusion Task Force, 2006a, 2006b, 2008).

Research at the Cassel Hospital has indicated that adults who have had abusing experiences in childhood, and who respond to these experiences by an inhibition of reflective function, are less likely to resolve their abuse, and are also more likely to manifest borderline pathology. If the abused child or adult has access to a relationship that can help them deal with the emotional impact of their abuse, they can, to some degree, resolve the experience; they may then be protected from severe borderline pathology (Fonagy et al., 1996).

Therapeutic communities have a long track record of working psychotherapeutically to engage and heal the damaged minds of most excluded, traumatized, and abused adults and children (National Institute for Mental Health in England [NIMHE], 2003).

Childhood First

Childhood First (formerly known as the Peper Harow Foundation) is a pioneer in the field of group-based psychodynamic and systemic care. We are a charity that has been successfully healing severely disturbed children and young people for over 35 years.

Childhood First treats the most severely damaged children and young people in the Looked After Sector and achieves results which are in some areas as good as mainstream non-looked after children and young people.

The children's and young people's lives have been thrown off-course by early life trauma: neglect, deprivation or abuse. The consequences of these early experiences manifest in a range of emotional states, which can include feelings of mistrust, anger, panic or worthlessness. Outward symptoms can be aggressive, disruptive or self-harming behaviour, and an inability to form appropriate relationships and attachments.

The majority of the children and young people in our centres have been in local authority care, and many have experienced numerous care and family placements before referral to us. In many cases these children have been referred to us in consultation with psychotherapists and psychiatrists—some young people come to us directly from psychiatric units.

Our work is based on psychodynamic principles, and our centres work with troubled and vulnerable children and young people to help them to overcome their traumatic experiences. The care which we offer includes regular group and individual staff supervision from consultant psychotherapists or psychiatrists: this informs the work with the children.

We run residential communities, which offer non-secure, consent-based, group-based, therapeutic care, education and treatment. We also provide family and placement support services to help vulnerable children with complex needs. We aim to help young people to make sense of the past, and give them a different experience of being "parented" in the present, helping them to look forward to a future in which they can take responsibility for their own lives. Our approach helps children to learn to build stable and healthy relationships. Our residential centres care for children in group settings, enabling them to gain an appreciation of the responsibility each person has towards others, and the contribution which each individual is able to make to a community. Every child takes part in regular group meetings, and is made to feel that his or her opinion is valued and considered. We also pay very careful attention to all the details of children's surroundings and daily routines, building comfort and stability into every day's schedule. We provide homes, not institutions. Children in our centres may have been deprived of the basic skills which most people take for granted. We work to help them develop the abilities which we all need to survive in society. We see education as a fundamental part of each young person's life: our therapeutic staff work closely with teachers, whether education is provided as an integral part of on-site provision or at a mainstream or special needs school.

The severity of early adversity and its affects on subsequent emotional and social development is described in the following statistics:

Family history:

89% victims of serious abuse or neglect

39% victims of sexual abuse (20% by father; 17% by mother; 13% unknown abuser)

24% witness to sexual abuse

78% victims of domestic violence

51% victims of abuse and neglect before age 5

57% parents/carers involved in drug, alcohol, or substance misuse

50% parents/carers suffering psychiatric disorder/serious mental illness

63% have no contact with birth mothers

78% have no contact with birth fathers.

Placement history:

30% of the children who come to us have had more than 7 placement changes in their lives; 14% have had more than 11 placement
changes.

Preceding placements:

Overall: 36% foster care; 33% residential care; 12% psychiatric unit.

Thornby Hall: 26% psychiatric unit; 39% residential care.)

Presenting problems prior to admission:

84% conduct disorders

44% hyperkinetic disorders

90% emotional disorders—e.g. anorexia, self-harm

48% sexual behaviour not within range for normal for their age.

Educational continuity:

51% Permanently or temporarily excluded from school

25% Permanently excluded from school

19% Not attended school or any other educational provision prior
to admission

55% Statement of Special Educational Needs. [Blunden & Carter,
2007]

Therapeutic communities are able to work with such difficulties
through a theoretical understanding of the damaged mind, derived
from psychoanalysis, and systems and attachment theory (Blunden
& Carter 2007; Kennedy, Heymans, & Tischler, 1987; Warren &
Dolan, 2001).

The Cassel Hospital

The Cassel Hospital is an NHS national specialist service for the
assessment and treatment of adults, young people and families

with intractable personality and family problems. It offers effective treatment to people who have exhausted other avenues of help from mental health, children's and social care services. Since 1919 it has been a pioneer in the inpatient psychotherapeutic treatment of psychiatric disorders.

The Family Service at the Cassel Hospital provides inpatient psychotherapy for families where concern has been raised that the children cannot live safely at home. Almost invariably the difficulties of the parents in providing a safe environment for their children can only be fully understood through psychotherapeutic exploration of the traumatic or abusive experiences that the parents themselves experienced as children, and which gave them a distorted experience of parenting relationships and being parented. Facing the reality of past relationships and the emotional experiences of their childhoods, through the psychotherapy and psychosocial nursing programme is a cornerstone of enabling these parents to escape from their pasts and develop the capacity to parent their children in a safe way. [Kennedy, Heymans, & Tischler, 1987]

A review of the research on the intergenerational transmission of child abuse and abusive parenting found that about one third of children who have been subjected to abusive parenting went on to repeat patterns of abusive parenting towards their own children. One third of children did not, and a further third remained vulnerable, depending on environmental circumstances and stresses, to repeating their abusive experiences of parenting towards their own children (Oliver, 1993).

The same review found that while child victims of abuse tend to blame themselves, the single most important modifying factor identified in the intergenerational transmission of child abuse was the capacity of the child victim to grow up with the ability to face the reality of past and present relationships (*ibid.*).

This finding has been repeated many times. A number of studies have found that the crucial difference is that mothers who are trapped in a pattern of denial of their abusive experiences and idealization of their abusive parents were most likely to repeat the pattern of abusive parenting with their own children. Mothers who were able to break the cycle and not repeat with their children the abuses that they experienced, tended to be the ones who could recall their own abusive experiences as children in detail and with emotion (Egeland, Jacobvitz, & Papatola, 1987; Egeland, Jacobvitz, & Sroufe, 1988; Healy, Kennedy, & Sinclair, 1991; Sroufe, Egeland, Carlson, & Collins, 2005).

One large regional study of "problem families" where abuse was transmitted from generation to generation found that these families faced multiple adversities: parental mental health problems, personality disorder, misuse of drugs and alcohol, criminality, organic brain disorders, and mild learning disability. In one third of these families child abuse was known to have spanned three generations or more. These families accounted for 10% of cases of child abuse in the geographical region. The maltreating parents in these families often gave bland or idealized pictures of their own biological parents, especially their mothers, which were incompatible with old written records, to the extent of repeated omission of any knowledge of previously damaged or institutionalized children from the families (Oliver, 1988).

Kids Company

Kids Company was founded in December 1996 in order to provide practical and emotional support for "lone children". These are children and young people who experience significant psychosocial difficulties because their parent is unable to function as a caring adult. The lack of a functioning adult has a negative impact on their ability to access education, health, housing and meaningful employment.

The organization is advanced in its service delivery because it has a multidisciplinary team working at street level, adapting the latest neurophysiological thinking in order to deliver a preventative and reparative therapeutic service to children. The organization works in 32 very deprived inner-city schools across London. A holistic social work, psychotherapy, health therapy and arts programme is delivered to some 11,000 clients within the schools. Some of the children receive multiple services and therefore benefit from having all their needs met in school. Therapy rooms are set up so children are given the opportunity to ask for help directly, without having to rely on an adult to take them to appointments.

Work with 925+ exceptionally vulnerable children and young people: This vulnerable cohort of children have self-referred to Kids Company's day centres. They are youngsters whose parents have abandoned them. Many have been drug couriers, members of gangs, or in prostitution. The majority are addicted to hard drugs, arrive homeless and/or have identifiable mental health problems. They present with erratic or non-existent employment history, school exclusions and imprisonment. Having fallen through statutory care, they are often banned due to violence. They become perverse leaders, escalating violence in otherwise well cared-for peers who try to survive them. Prolonged drug use will lead to psychosis and local mental health provisions cannot cope. The lifestyles of these young people mean they cannot comply with medication and they continue to generate chaos.

These children use Kids Company's *Arches* programme (situated in Lambeth) like a substitute family environment. The majority attend six days a week. All their needs are met on site through a team of psychologists, nurses, a GP, social workers, alternative health therapists, teachers, employment advisers, youth offending workers, arts therapists and key workers. The aim of the Arches is to provide the children with a family experience which helps repair their sense of abandonment and work through their traumas; a legacy of their being subjected to sexual and physical abuse. These are the children that local authorities find difficult to manage, because their behaviour is so disturbed and their needs so complex.

Health: Kids Company delivers an extensive mental and physical health programme. In the 32 inner-city schools, we provide one-to-one therapy, group therapy, counselling for parents and teachers, nutritional therapy, homeopathy, massage and reflexology. Children who are psychiatrically ill are assisted through the referral system to see a psychiatrist within the NHS. Within the schools programme, approximately 7,000 children per annum are supported in health and psychotherapy interventions.

Statistics pertaining to Kids Company's client group compiled by the University of London evaluation include: 84% homelessness; 81% criminal involvement; 87% emotional difficulties; 82% substance misuse; 83% had sustained trauma; 39% are teenage carers.

Independent analysis of 10 Kids Company children's files revealed: 9 out of 10 had drug and alcohol addictions; all the children had worked with local youth offending teams with limited success; 6 of the children had been sexually abused; 4 of the children made repeated suicide attempts.

Crime Concern Independent Evaluation 2003 identified Kids Company as having an 85% success rate in reintegrating excluded pupils into mainstream education, compared to the national average of 34%. [Gaskell, 2008]

Trafficked children

Child trafficking is covert and highly varied; the true extent of child trafficking is unknown. In 2006, the Home Office commissioned the Child Exploitation and Online Protection Centre to conduct an intelligence-gathering project to try to establish the level of existing information and understanding of child trafficking. This found that:

Traffickers target children who are already relatively vulnerable. Trafficked children have come from broken families or destitute circumstances within their own countries. Those trafficked from the different parts of Africa for sexual exploitation and domestic servitude came from the most destitute backgrounds. They described their previous lives in terms of bereavement, being orphaned, victims or prisoners of war, victims of sexual and physical abuse, forced into marriages, female genital mutilation, victims of police brutality, prison and witnessing murder. Most of these children came from poor families with little access to education (CEOP, 2007).

> A girl was trafficked from Albania to Italy and into prostitution. The traffickers brutally raped and beat her, forcing her to use drugs until she became addicted. At one point she was recovered by the Italian authorities and returned to the Albanian authorities, only to be sold back to another set of traffickers. This time the traffickers brought her to the UK and forced her back into prostitution. [*ibid.*, p. 23]

For most trafficked children, the type of exploitation into which they are being trafficked is not clear. Some children reported having been exploited in more than one type of exploitation.

The type of exploitation was known for 49% of trafficked girls. Of these girls, 66% were trafficked for sexual exploitation and 24% were trafficked for domestic servitude.

The type of exploitation was known for only 8% of trafficked boys. These boys were trafficked for cannabis cultivation, labour exploitation, domestic servitude, begging, and benefit fraud.

Research into the specific conditioning and psychological effects of trafficking on boys is even less available than for girls.

Physical and sexual violence is a common occurrence in the trafficking of children. For almost all girls trafficked for sexual exploitation, violence and sexual violence is the primary method used by traffickers for maintaining control. Girls are raped repeatedly until they are compliant and then prostituted. They describe being repeatedly raped and gang raped, physically beaten, injured, and burnt by cigarettes. Often they are beaten in front of each other in order to instil fear in the whole group. Some described witnessing murder committed by their traffickers. They are coerced by threats to harm their families back at home. Addiction to drugs is also used to control girls trafficked for sexual exploitation.

> A woman was trafficked to Italy into prostitution as a girl. Subsequently, she was trafficked to the UK and was "pimped" for many years. She had been made a drug addict in order for her "pimp" to maintain control. She was physically and sexually abused on a regular basis and when she became ill and "unattractive" she was "pimped" out on the streets. After seven years of exploitation she came to the attention of the authorities. She had scaring [sic] from injections and cigarette butt burns on her body and was in a terrible psychological state. [ibid., p. 33]

Children trafficked for sexual exploitation are subject to the most severe forms of sexual violence. However, children in domestic servitude also regularly report being sexually abused, raped, and physically abused in the homes in which they are exploited.

Many children were trafficked when they were much younger and had been exploited for years. Some children in domestic servitude were trafficked as young as seven years of age, and only came to the attention of the authorities when they were older and able to seek help.

Some of the girls believed they were being rescued from their destitution and still refer to these persons who brought them to the UK as their rescuers. Some children reported being in exploitation within their home countries, including prostitution and domestic servitude. Children reported suffering from domestic abuse in their families before falling victim to trafficking.

Children who have been trafficked and exploited need appropriate and specialized care and support. Trafficked children often have a history of abuse and vulnerability.

In addition to the original abuse and vulnerability of the child's background, trafficking and exploitation would have had additional traumatic effects on the child.

The traumas of trafficking, violence, sexual violence, exploitation, drug addiction, and pre-existing abuse, deprivation, neglect, and loss, multiply each other's effects.

Some children who have been trafficked felt that they were not treated the same as children who were British born. Some reported that some children's services approached them from an immigration status, rather than a child protection point of view, thereby perpetuating rejection and neglect.

What is appropriate care depends on the child, and his or her background: abuse and neglect suffered before the trafficking situation may have a deeper affect on trafficked children than their subsequent exploitation.

These children will require access to a full range of psychotherapeutic treatments. These psychotherapies will need to be adapted to the individuals' needs and circumstances and be available long-term.

Under-reporting

Non-disclosure of sexual abuse is the norm. One retrospective community study found that only 10% of women who had experienced childhood sexual abuse had reported it to the police, a doctor, or a helping agency (Fleming, 1997).

There are significant barriers to the reporting of sexual abuse of disabled children to the authorities. It is estimated that only three per cent of sexual abuse cases involving people with developmental disabilities will ever be reported. Other estimates are that 75% of abuse cases involving disabled victims are not reported to the authorities (Sobsey & Varnhagen, 1989; Valenti-Hein & Schwartz, 1995). Even when a crime is reported few cases are taken to Court or result in a conviction (Hewitt, 1987; James & Nasjleti, 1983; O'Day, 1983). People with disabilities do not make attractive clients for some lawyers. Police may be reluctant to take action because people with a learning disability may not be considered as competent or reliable witnesses (Buchanan & Wilkins, 1991).

Boys and men are also less likely to report sexual abuse (see "Gender and child sexual abuse", below).

> Linda, an eight-year-old severely learning disabled girl, masturbated with a toothbrush every evening in her foster-home. She wet the bed each night and displayed a great deal of emotional disturbance after each access visit to her parents. The foster-mother was convinced that sexual abuse was taking place at the girl's home but no professional believed her. Indeed, one professional firmly stated, "On no account should this child's hypersexual activity be seen as anything other than intrinsic to her brain damage". Only when the child's desperate communications extended to her school classroom was a referral made to a child abuse team. At interview with a psychotherapist specializing in learning disability, sexual abuse was disclosed. As a result, contact with the abusing parents was stopped. She received weekly psychodynamic psychotherapy and her sexualized behaviour diminished.

Online abuse

Online chat rooms and social networking sites give new opportunities for paedophiles to groom potential victims online for inappropriate or abusive relationships, which may include requests to make and transmit pornographic images of themselves, or to perform sexual acts live in front of a web cam. There is also growing cause for concern about the exposure of children to adult pornography and extreme forms of obscene material (Department for Education and Skills, 2006). The Internet allows the dissemination of images of child sexual abuse. The Child Exploitation and Online Protection Centre was launched in 2006, and has multiple roles in protecting children from online abuse through education, identification, law enforcement, and improving preventative measures (www.ceop.gov.uk).

Gender, violence, and abuse

Gender is closely linked to levels of domestic violence, and physical and sexual abuse. A historical concern about violence committed by men against women has led researchers and feminists to draw attention to male perpetrators and female victims. Arguably, however, this has led to the needs of female perpetrators and male victims being overlooked. In recent years, the research literature has included studies of both male and female violence and sexual offending.

Gender and domestic violence

Domestic violence covers a wide range of severity. In 2001–2002, in England and Wales, 116 women and thirty-two men were killed by a current or former partner (Flood-Page & Taylor, 2003).

Domestic violence is very common. The British Crime Survey, in England and Wales, indicates that domestic violence now accounts for 16% of all violent crime; one in four women and one in six men will be a victim of domestic violence at some point in their lives. However, between 1995 and 2004–2005, the BCS recorded a 59% fall in domestic violence (Nicholas, Povey, Walker, & Kershaw, 2005).

Historically, domestic violence has been considered as something that men do to women, and much research has only considered violence by men against women (Strauss, 1993). Part of the reason for this may be that women are more likely to report domestic violence than men. One study found that, in the same sample of couples, 28% of women, but only 19% of men, reported that their relationships were violent (Whitaker, Haileyesus, Swahn, & Saltzman, 2007). A study of non-consensual sexual experiences in men found that fewer than three per cent of these experiences were reported to police (Coxell, King, Mezey, & Gordon, 1999).

However, in recent years large epidemiological studies have demonstrated that domestic violence is commonly reciprocal, and that when only one partner is violent there is an excess of violent women (Archer, 2000; Strauss, 1993, 2001; Whitaker, Haileyesus, Swahn, & Saltzman, 2007).

Among 14,000 young adults in the USA, about a quarter of relationships were violent, and in half of the relationships the violence was reciprocal; both women and men reported that in non-reciprocal domestic violence, 70% of the aggressors were women. The highest rate of injury was men against women in reciprocally violent relationships (31.4%) (Whitaker, Haileyesus, Swahn, & Saltzman, 2007).

A meta-analysis of eighty-two studies of sex differences in physical aggression to heterosexual partners found that men were more likely to inflict an injury; 62% of those injured by a partner were women. However, women were slightly more likely than men to use one or more act of physical aggression and to use such acts more frequently. Younger-aged couples showed more female aggression (Archer, 2000).

The US National Comorbidity Survey demonstrated severe physical aggression against 6.5% of women and against 5.5% of men (Kessler, Molnar, Feurer, & Appelbaum, 2001).

Among couples seeking marital therapy, 64% of wives and 61% of husbands were classified as aggressive (Langhinrichsen-Rohling & Vivian, 1994).

In 272 engaged couples, 44% of women and 31% of men reported physical violence towards their partners (O'Leary et al., 1989).

Among women, risks of domestic violence do not differ significantly by ethnic origin. The risk of domestic violence to men does, however, vary by ethnic group. White men are more likely to be assaulted by their partner than men in other ethnic groups.

White men are as likely to be assaulted as white women. Asian men are significantly less likely to be assaulted than Asian women. Black men are intermediate. Women were attacked by men in 99% of cases. Men were attacked by women in 95% of cases (Mirrlees-Black, 1999).

People of all sexual orientations experience domestic violence in a similar proportion to the rest of the population. In a study of lesbians and gay men, 22% of lesbian women reported domestic violence from a previous female partner and 29% of gay men from a previous male partner (Henderson, 2003).

Gender and child sexual abuse

Data from population surveys and criminal statistics indicate that men commit the majority of recorded sexual offences. A Home

Office review found that women committed fewer than 5% of recorded sexual offences, but that community surveys suggested that the actual figure is higher (Grubin, 1998).

Much of the quantitative research on abuser characteristics comes from forensic populations. Individuals, whose sexual offending is recognized, reported, and results in conviction might differ substantially from the perpetrators of child sexual abuse that does not result in conviction.

Research on forensic populations of male abusers indicates that two thirds of offenders target girls only, about a quarter target boys only, and about one in ten target children of both sexes (Grubin, 1998).

A historic study of fifty-two convicted paedophiles found that, in 80% of offences, the victim was well known to the perpetrators and assaults occurred in the home of the perpetrator or victim (Bradford, Bloomberg, & Bourget, 1988).

About 20% of men convicted of a sexual offence are reconvicted for similar offences; this is lower than the recidivism rate for non-sexual crimes. However, there are subgroups of prolific offenders with substantially higher reoffending rates (Grubin, 1998).

Community surveys report higher rates of extra-familial abuse. A study of over 1200 students found that half of women and a quarter of men had experienced unwanted sexual encounters before the age of eighteen. The commonest reported events were flashing (27%) and touching (23%). Serious abuse (rape and forced masturbation) was experienced by 5% of women and 2% of men. Women were between two and three times more likely to experience sexual abuse than men. Over one quarter of assaults were committed by peers (under eighteen). Two per cent of the sample reported incestuous abuse. Half of these were abuse by fathers or stepfathers; the others by brothers, and in one case a sister. Other close family members abused a further 4%: grandfathers, uncles, and an aunt. Men committed most abuse. Female abusers were 15% in the peer abuse category and 5% in the adult category. Young men reported most of the events involving female abusers (Kelly, Regan, & Burton, 1991).

A recent review by the National Society for the Prevention of Cruelty to Children found that women commit up to five per cent of all sexual offences against children, often against their own children, and that the abuse can take overt and covert forms. The report identified institutional barriers to recognizing female-perpetrated abuse and a reluctance to recognize it among professionals (Bunting, 2007).

There is substantial research demonstrating the potential for female-perpetrated sexual abuse to be taken less seriously than male-perpetrated child sexual abuse (Bunting, 2007; Davies, Pollard, & Archer, 2006; Hetherton & Beardsall, 1998; Rogers & Davies, 2007). Boys having sexual experiences with adult women are more likely to regard these experiences as consensual or positive (Coxell, King, Mezey, & Gordon, 1999; Rind, Tromovitch, & Bauserman, 1998).

There is also a relative lack of research on treatment of female sexual offenders (Oliver, 2007).

There is a lack of co-ordinated strategy in the UK Criminal Justice System for assessing the risks posed by female sexual abusers, and this leads to a downgrading of risk. Furthermore, there is a danger that, when co-offending with a male partner, some female sexual abusers may be assigned the role of coerced victim on the basis of gender rather than evidence. Misconceptions about female sexuality and aggression are a barrier to the recognition of female-perpetrated abuse and the tendency to minimize female sexual offences may in itself contribute to low rates of reported abuse (Bunting, 2005, 2007).

Both Welldon and Kennedy have given detailed accounts of female abusers, and some of the barriers that prevent the recognition of female abusers (Kennedy, 1997; Welldon, 1988).

Adolescents and children who commit child sexual abuse

Adolescent sex offenders account for up to a third of recorded sex crime. Young abusers are a heterogeneous group (Bentovim & Williams, 1998). One quarter to one half of young abusers have learning disabilities (Hickey, Vizard, McCrory, & French, 2006).

Often, the sexual interests of young abusers are age appropriate and only a minority appear to have a sexual interest in children *per se*. It is thought that these child molesters are likely to become adult paedophiles (Grubin, 1998). However, much remains to be known about the range of "normal" adolescent sexuality (Lovell, 2002a).

A study of 280 juvenile sexual abusers (91% male) found that onset of sexually abusive behaviour before the age of eleven years was associated with inadequate family sexual boundaries, multiple forms of abuse and neglect, poorer parenting, difficult temperament, and insecure attachment; these children had a diverse range of victims. The children whose sexually abusive behaviour appeared after the age of eleven experienced more substance misuse, abused girls or much younger children, and were more likely to use verbal coercion. The parents of these young people were very troubled in their own right: as children the parents of 40% of the sample had been victims of abuse or neglect, 24% had spent time in Local Authority care, and 41% were judged to be suffering from mental disorders in adulthood. More than three quarters of the young abusers had been removed into Local Authority care (Hickey, Vizard, McCrory, & French, 2006).

A review by the NSPCC found similar results: nearly a third of the children referred to one of their projects for young people with sexually abusive behaviour were under ten years old; they were found to have particularly troubled backgrounds with physical and sexual abuse, substance misuse, emotional victimization, or abandonment, and high rates of psychiatric or learning disabilities and medical problems (Lovell, 2002b).

Attachment, trauma, dissociation, and the developing brain

Attachment

Attachment theory developed from psychoanalysis and ethology. It describes a core human need to form close affectional bonds, how these early relationships develop, and the role of these attachment relationships in subsequent development of the personality (Bowlby, 1969, 1973, 1980). Early reciprocal relationships are probably a precondition of survival and development in all mammals (Hofer, 1995).

Humans are born dependent on their parents for safety and survival. The survival of the child depends on the proximity of its parent. The survival of the human species has required that babies and their parents are able to elicit caring responses and proximity-seeking behaviours from each other. When danger threatens, the child seeks proximity to its attachment figure. These behaviours are thought initially to be genetically determined. Later, they are shaped by learning.

At birth, human infants are without the ability to regulate their arousal and emotional reactions. They cannot soothe or comfort themselves, nor can they maintain their physiological homoeostasis.

However, through the development of attachment bonds, a complex process of attunement takes place between infant and care-giver.

The attachment system not only provides protection for the infant, but it enables the development of psychobiological attunement between infant and care-giver, a process that provides, from birth onward, a matching of inner states between mother and infant described as "affect attunement" (Stern, 1985).

As development takes place, infants become alert to the physical and emotional availability of their care-givers, who might sometimes be either unpredictable or rejecting. These repeated experiences are synthesized in the infant's mind to become what Bowlby has called "internal working models" or internal representations of how the attachment figure is likely to respond to the child's attachment behaviour. These working models have been explored using the "strange situation" (Ainsworth, Blehar, Waters, & Wall, 1978).

The strange situation has allowed researchers to classify the different ways in which one-year-old infants responded to separation from their care-givers, depending on how secure their attachment was to that care-giver.

Attachment styles

Table 1 shows the classification of infants' behaviour in the strange situation at one year. In the strange situation the infant is observed playing in presence of the mother, who then leaves the infant twice, once in the presence of a stranger, and once alone. The quality of the child's behaviour on reunion with its mother is rated.

Reflective function

Subsequent studies using the adult attachment interview have shown that, if the care-giver or another important individual to

Table 1.   Infants' "strange situation" behaviour at one year.

Infant attachment style	Infant's behaviour	Mother's behaviour
Secure (B)*	Distressed at separation. Seeks mother on return, is quickly reassured and returns to play.	Sensitive and responsive.
Insecure avoidant (A)	Not distressed at separation. Doesn't seek mother on return (but shows highest levels of physiological stress).	Dismissive or interfering.
Insecure anxious/ ambivalent (C)	Seeks mother on return, but not reassured; clingy or indifferent.	Insensitive and unpredictable.
Insecure disorganized (D)[†]	Grossly disorganized behaviour; apprehensive in presence of mother.	Appears frightened or frightening.

*Securely attached children are resilient to later trauma and stress.
[†]Children with the D pattern of attachment are at increased risk of psychiatric disorder.

whom the child is attached demonstrates "reflective functioning" by giving meaning to the infant's experiences and sharing and predicting his or her behaviour, the child can internalize this capacity (Fonagy & Target, 1997).

Such a developmental acquisition is described as "reflective functioning" or "mentalization", which enables people to understand each other in terms of mental states and intentions. It is key to developing a sense of agency and continuity as well as enabling people to interact successfully with others. It also protects children from some of the deleterious effects of abuse by reducing their risk of re-enacting past traumatic experiences.

A securely attached child has a mental representation of the caregiver as responsive in times of trouble. Such children feel confident, and are capable of empathy and of forming good attachments. The good enough mother of the securely attached infant is accessible to the child in need and shows a tendency to respond appropriately to her child's positive and negative emotional expressions.

These regulated events allow for the expansion of the child's capacity to regulate his or her emotions and account for the principle that security of the attachment bond is the primary defence against trauma-induced psychopathology (Schore, 2002).

In the securely attached individual, the attachment representation encodes an implicit expectation that homoeostatic disruptions will be set right, allowing the child to self-regulate functions that previously required the care-giver's external regulation (Schore, 1996).

Insecure and disorganized attachment

Insecure attachments develop when the infants do not have a mental representation of a responsive care-giver in times of need, such as when they feel fearful or helpless. These infants develop different strategies to gain access to their care-giver in order to survive.

Two types of organized insecure attachment behaviours have been recognized using the "strange situation" (Ainsworth, Blehar, Waters, & Wall, 1978), and a third pattern of disorganized attachment behaviour has been subsequently recognized (Main & Hess, 1992):

1. infants who show an anxious-ambivalent response;
2. infants who show an avoidant type of response;
3. infants who show a disorganized response.

About 15% of one-year-old infants in non-clinical, low-risk, and up to 80% in high-risk (e.g., maltreated) populations show extensive disorganized attachment behaviour (Main & Solomon, 1990; van Ijzendoorn, Schuengel, & Bakermans-Kranenburg, 1999).

Infants with disorganized attachment show an unpredictable response in relation to their care-giver and are seen to freeze in a trance-like state, very much like adult sufferers of post traumatic stress disorder.

For those whose early experiences have meant fear, in particular fear without solution, such as is observed in infants with a "disorganized" attachment pattern, care-givers demonstrate not only less affect attunement, but they also induce traumatic states of enduring negative affect in the child, either by frightening or by being frightened. These children might have a history of maltreatment and/or parents with a history of abuse or unresolved loss (Liotti, 1995).

The infant will have limited opportunity to experience the reflection of its own mind in its mother's mind. The child will, therefore, have little opportunity to find out about its own mind. Deprived of this experience, the child will have an impaired sense of his own emotional states, and emotional life reflective functioning will be impaired. The child may mirror its mother's disturbed emotional states and identify with her emotional states as if they were its own (Schore, 2003; Fonagy, Gergely, Jurist, & Target, 2004).

The loss of ability to regulate the intensity of emotions may be the most far-reaching effect of early trauma and neglect (van der Kolk, 1996).

Trauma and dissociation

The infant's psychobiological response to trauma comprises two separate response patterns: hyper-arousal and dissociation.

Initially, the fight/flight response is mediated by the sympathetic nervous system. The level of arousal blocks the reflective symbolic processing, with the result that traumatic experiences are stored in sensory, somatic, behavioural, and affective systems (Perry et al., 1995).

If the fight/flight response is not possible, a parasympathetic state takes over and the child "freezes", which, in nature, may be linked to feigning death and thereby fostering survival (Solms & Turnbull, 2002). Vocalization is also inhibited. Like young animals, human beings can lose the capacity to speak: a phenomenon that is related to the release of endogenous opiates and observed in the PET scans on patients with post traumatic stress disorder (Rauch et al., 1996).

In enduring traumatic states of helplessness, or "fear without solution", both of the above responses are activated, leading to an "inward flight" or dissociative response.

Children in fear of their care-givers' hatred and violence will maintain their attachment to their desperately needed care-giver by resorting to processes that are generally referred to by psychoanalysts as *splitting* and by neuropsychologists as *dissociation*. Splitting and dissociation are related concepts. For a discussion of similarities and differences see Scharff & Scharff (1994). In splitting or dissociation, children create different mental representations of themselves in relation to their care-givers.

This involves the child dividing his mind into separate parts, creating different images of himself and his care-giver: in the child's mind, there might then be a good parent whom the child can rely on, with a good child who is loved by the parent, but also, separated off—*split off* or *dissociated*—there is another image of a bad parent who abuses him, and a bad child.

These contradictory and incompatible representations of self and the parent or care-giver lead to a lack of a clear sense of self, or sense of continuity in others. This lack of self-continuity is seen in patients with a borderline personality disorder (Fonagy & Target, 1997; Ryle, 1997; de Zulueta, 1999).

Even if childhood trauma does not result in enduring use of dissociation, abuse undermines the child's capacities to reflect on his or her own desires or fantasies or to contemplate what may be in the mind of his or her parents, if this implies the contemplation of the all-too-real wishes of the parent to harm the child (Bollas, 1987; Fonagy, Steele, & Steele, 1991). This interferes with the development of capacities for self-reflection, and that ability to think in terms of mental states of self and others. These deficiencies in self-reflection and mentalization are thought to underlie the pathogenesis of borderline personality disorder (Fonagy, Gergely, Jurist, & Target, 2004).

A nineteen-year-long follow-up study of infants with a disorganized attachment showed a tendency to develop dissociative disorders in adulthood ranging from borderline personality disorder to dissociative identity disorders (Ogawa, Sroufe, Weinfield, Carlson, & Egeland, 1997).

By dissociating or splitting off the experiences and memories of their terrifying interactions with the care-giver the infant will develop an idealized image of the care-giver in order to maintain the attachment to him or her.

At a cognitive level, these children blame themselves for their suffering, and thereby retain the idealized version of their care-giver as well as retaining a sense of control. They believe that they them-selves are the cause of their misery and, therefore, one day, if they manage to behave better, they may finally get the love and care that they need. This *moral defence* is a powerful one and is main-tained because not only does it ward off the sense of utter help-lessness that humans cannot bear, but it also gives the individual hope of something better (Fairbairn, 1952). Unfortunately, it also reinforces the attachment and identification with the abusing parent. Addressing this "traumatic attachment" and its cognitive distortions is central to the treatment of patients with a history of child abuse. A similar cognitive distortion takes place in adults suffering from late-onset trauma, but it is more accessible to modifi-cation.

Once dissociation has been established, during the preschool period, as a way of dealing with maltreatment, children thereafter might follow a different developmental trajectory, with the amount of dissociation increasing through the preschool period, as com-pared to children who have not been maltreated, who show no such increase. Increasing use of dissociation is thought to interfere with the normal development, and integrated sense, of self. This failure to achieve integration of the self is linked with subsequent distur-bance throughout the life-cycle, with cascading implications for subsequent development (MacFie, Cicchetti, & Toth, 2001).

Attachment in adults

Attachment style is one of the principle determinants of resilience to later trauma; it predicts how well children will cope with life's difficulties and if they will develop mental illness. It also predicts how, as adults, they will treat their children, and the sort of attach-ment their children will develop (Fonagy, Steele, & Steele, 1991). In this way, styles of attachment are transmitted across generations.

Insecure or disorganized attachment can be overcome if the patient is able to develop and experience a secure attachment in his or her life. For some, this will only happen in a psychotherapeutic relationship.

One of the goals of psychoanalytic psychotherapy is to modify attachment style, in order that people can learn to recognize their emotional distress for what it is, and seek and accept caring from those around them appropriately; in other words, to develop secure attachment.

Deep-seated trauma requires sustained treatment in depth over time to effect change. An integrated personality and capacity to form secure attachments is a hard-won developmental achievement for the patient who has experienced severe traumatization.

Dissociative disorders

If the reliance on dissociation is excessive, it might reach the level of severity of a disorder. There is a continuum of dissociative disorders:

- depersonalization and derealization;
- dissociative amnesia;
- dissociative fugue;
- dissociative identity disorder (multiple personality disorder).

A study in a British psychiatric inpatient unit estimated a 15% prevalence rate for dissociative disorders (Aquarone & Hughes, 2005).

People who have experienced severe trauma and who dissociate into two or more personalities for emotional survival may fulfil the criteria for a diagnosis of a dissociative identity disorder, in the classification of the *Diagnostic and Statistical Manual* (*DSM-IV*) of the American Psychiatric Association (2000), or multiple personality disorder, as described in the *International Classification of Diseases* (*ICD-10*) of the World Health Organization (1992).

Post traumatic stress disorder, although not classified as a dissociative disorder, shares many features with the other dissociative disorders, and is common in people with dissociative identity disorder.

Although, historically, there has been debate over the existence and true prevalence of dissociative identity disorder, it is a valid diagnostic entity that can be reliably diagnosed (Gabbard, 2005). However it is under-diagnosed in Britain and Europe (Friedl & Draijer, 2000; Friedl, Draijer, & de Jonge, 2000).

Studies in North America demonstrate a prevalence of 1–3% in the general population (Murphy, 1994; Ross, 1991; Waller & Ross,

1997). Studies in psychiatric clinical populations in North America, Europe, and Turkey reveal rates of 1–20% (Bliss & Jeppsen, 1985; Goff, Olin, Jenike, Baer, & Buttolph, 1992; Latz, Kramer, & Highes, 1995; McCallum, Lock, Kulla, Rorty, & Wetzel, 1992; Modestin, Ebner, Junghan, & Erni, 1995; Ross, Anderson, Fleisher, & Norton, 1991; Ross et al., 1992; Saxe et al., 1993; Tutkun et al., 1998).

Dissociative identity disorder in DSM-IV/Multiple personality disorder in ICD-10

A. The presence of two or more distinct identities or personality states (each with its own relatively enduring pattern of perceiving, relating to, and thinking about the environment and self).
B. At least two of these identities or personality states recurrently take control of the person's behaviour.
C. Inability to recall important personal information that is too extensive to be explained by ordinary forgetfulness.
D. Not due to the direct effects of a substance (e.g., blackouts or chaotic behaviour during alcohol intoxication) or a general medical condition (e.g., complex partial seizures)

Ninety per cent of patients meeting the *DSM-IV* criteria for dissociative identity disorder provide a history of physical and sexual abuse (Fonagy & Target, 1995). However, it is not the case that all people who have been abused show dissociation.

From age three until early adulthood Ms F was severely abused: sexually, physically and emotionally by multiple perpetrators, included [*sic*] incest by both parents, ritual abuse within a satanic cult and forced prostitution. She was first admitted to psychiatric care as an inpatient at the age of seventeen, and for the next twenty-two years she was a "revolving door" patient. During much of this period the abuse was ongoing but unrecognised by a range of mental health professionals.

Her diagnosis changed repeatedly. Diagnoses included anxiety disorder, clinical depression, borderline personality disorder, atypical manic depression and schizophrenia, but neither the impact of abuse nor a diagnosis of PTSD or complex dissociative disorder was ever considered. Treatments included different medications, electric shock treatment (ECT), non-trauma-focused psychotherapy and even a period living in a therapeutic community. None of these treatments was effective in the long term, and most were ineffective even in the shorter term. At the age of thirty-nine, Ms F sought help in the independent sector from a psychotherapist who used an eclectic approach based primarily on psychoanalytical and systemic ideas. After an extended assessment the therapist suspected Ms F had dissociative identity disorder. This diagnosis was subsequently confirmed by an NHS psychiatrist.

The therapy specifically addressed her myriad dissociative defences, including the different "selves" she had developed through using dissociation to survive the abuse as a child.

Gradually, as trust developed, Ms F's extreme history of trauma was addressed as each of the dissociated "selves" spontaneously shared their fragments of the whole history. Much of the therapeutic work focused on the relationship between therapist and client.

Ms F worked with her therapist for a number of years. When therapy ended she had a better and more integrated understanding of what had happened in her past; dissociative episodes (and therefore many of the symptoms that had brought her into psychiatric care) were less disruptive to her life and she had developed healthier ways of coping when they did occur. In her own terms her recovery continues but she does now have a happier, more balanced and well adjusted life.

The presence of pre-existing disorganized attachment may explain why some children are more prone to use dissociation to survive extreme trauma than other children.

Post traumatic stress disorder

Post traumatic stress disorder could be seen as a manifestation of a disrupted attachment system and, for this reason, has very serious implications in terms of family life. When examining the characteristic symptoms, one finds clear similarities between them and the psychobiological manifestations of a disrupted attachment system.

One mother who suffered from PTSD came to clinic with a small girl who showed failure to thrive. The mother had been severely beaten by the child's father. When the little girl became distressed her eyes resembled those of her father, eliciting in the mother a fear response rather than the comforting behaviour the child required. [de Zulueta, 2006]

The overwhelming flashbacks of post traumatic stress disorder are dissociative phenomena. This appears to result from the failure to integrate trauma into the declarative memory system. Trauma then remains organized at a sensory and somatic level, and the traumatic response can be unconsciously triggered and physically re-experienced without the conscious memories to accompany it. This represents a somatic form of dissociation.

The traumatized individual is repeatedly exposed to states of high arousal that cannot be handled due to an associated inability to modulate such experiences, both biologically and psychologically. Attempts are then made to self-medicate the pain and dysphoria with drugs or alcohol (van der Kolk, 1996).

Diagnostic criteria for post traumatic stress disorder are based on observations of people who have experienced circumscribed traumatic events. Children and adults exposed to repeated, protracted, interpersonal trauma show disturbances that are not captured in the post traumatic stress disorder diagnosis.

DSM-IV-TR refers to a constellation of symptoms that are more commonly seen in association with an interpersonal stressor (such as childhood sexual or physical abuse or neglect) (American Psychiatric Association, 2000). These include:

- impaired affect modulation leading to self-destructive and impulsive behaviour;
- dissociative symptoms;
- somatic complaints;
- feelings of ineffectiveness, shame, guilt, despair, hopelessness, feeling permanently damaged;
- hostility, social withdrawal, feeling constantly threatened, impaired relationships with others;
- a change from the person's previous personality characteristics.

This combination of symptoms has been referred to as complex PTSD, or, alternatively, as disorder of extreme stress (Herman, 1992; van der Kolk, Roth, Pelcovitz, Sunday, & Spinazzola, 2005).

The journey

- Severe child sexual abuse may require a lifetime process of recovery.
- Psychotherapy needs to be available long term and open ended.
- At different life stages survivors will have different needs.
- The need, ability, and desire to use psychotherapy will change over time.
- The opportunity to return for top-ups of psychotherapy is important.
- Survivor groups and literature are important.
- Vulnerability is increased at certain times: puberty, starting and ending sexual relationships, pregnancy, childbirth, bereavement, etc.
- Some groups may have more difficulty accessing psychotherapy, e.g., men, black and ethnic minorities, and the disabled.
- Psychoanalytic psychotherapy will not be the first choice for everyone, but it needs to be available.

People who have experienced sexual abuse, violence and neglect may need to access different services at different stages in their life.

The connections between the abusive experiences and current difficulties may or may not be clear to the individual or to professionals
offering help for physical problems. Sometimes abusive experiences
may be forgotten, and are recovered later. See "Recovered memories" above.

Voluntary and independent sector services provide a wide
range of services, including social support, mutual support, and
self-help groups, which can be more accessible and flexible than
statutory services and can help an individual to build up to and
maintain engagement with more intensive psychotherapy.

> Erica entered a two-year individual therapy contract and remained
> in therapy until the end of the contract. She approached the Centre
> at a time when she was feeling very depressed. She talked of how
> she had . . . stopped functioning . . . lost so much confidence, had
> become nervous, was not socialising and was spending a lot of time
> in her flat alone. Alongside this she was not coping in her work-
> place. Her work involved communicating with and supporting
> others and she had reached a point where she was struggling to
> . . . pick up the phone and call people. As well as coping with diffi-
> culties from her childhood, including parental neglect and a sexual
> relationship with a sibling, she had recently experienced violence
> from a partner and had been involved in a serious accident. Of the
> latter she felt that they had . . . shook me up so much and that she
> had . . . never felt so bad in my whole life. At the time of approach-
> ing the Centre she spoke of feeling nervous and different. Whilst
> Erica remained in therapy until the completion of her contract, she
> found the process of being in therapy frequently perplexing. At the
> time of the interview she spoke of how the therapy process had
> only begun to make sense during the last six months of the two
> years and since . . . it wasn't until I left again that I realised how
> much it had helped me. When reflecting on what she felt that she
> gained from therapy, she spoke of how she now felt less depressed,
> more confident, more able to view herself as worth caring about . .
> . more able to say no to others and more able to tell others what she
> truly thought. In addition she talked of how she had learned
> through therapy to take full responsibility for her life and her
> future and to move forward beyond the difficulties she had experi-
> enced in both her childhood and adult life . . . you have to learn
> how to live regardless. These "internal" outcomes appeared to have
> led to a shift in her "external" world. She spoke of how she now

was able to form stronger friendships . . . I moved on in terms of friendship . . . much better quality of friendships . . . I left some people behind. She had also left a job that she had felt stuck in and was in the process of pursuing a new career via embarking on a degree course . . . it [therapy] gave me the positivity to change. Further she had given up both nicotine and marijuana since being in therapy, had bought her own flat and had got married to a man with whom she felt she had developed a very positive relationship. Erica had experience of therapy prior to the Centre. She had started with several individual counsellors but had not stuck with the process. She also had had a positive experience of a two-year therapy group. At the time of the research interview, Erica did not feel that she currently required further therapy, but felt that if she did she would return to the Centre. However, she felt very unsure about whether she was prepared to . . . open it up again. Erica felt so positive about her experience at the Centre that she spoke of how she often had to hold herself back from telling others that they might benefit also. [Women's Therapy Centre, 2005]

People who have been abused frequently wish to dip in and out of services according to the level of adversity, distress, or support that they experience. Voluntary sector services may be seen as less stigmatizing, and more user-friendly.

I never told anyone what had happened to me until I was in my mid-forties. Until that point my partner and friends had no inkling of the secret that I had carried with me all my life. I had a successful career, a happy marriage and was, on the surface, outgoing and assertive.

But on the inside I felt very differently. I was waiting, constantly on alert for my secret to be found out. I found it difficult to trust people and had sleep problems and other physical ailments now readily identified as being stress induced.

My body, for decades, had lived on a knife-edge, on high alert.

I am one of five children, and was sexually abused by my father from the age of ten until I was 15½ when I managed to leave home. In September 1994 I was devastated to discover that I was not the only family member to have been sexually abused.

Even though our abuser was dead by that time, the impact on me was massive. The enormity of what had happened to me over-whelmed me. I was swallowed up by a continuous stream of flash-

backs replaying the ugliness of my childhood: the theft of inno-
cence through escalating abuses with rapes on a daily basis towards
the end; the physicality of the onslaught on my small, defenceless,
body; the inevitability of pregnancy and, following a suicide
attempt, the nightmare of the miscarriage (trying to ram the small
foetus down the bath plughole before finally flushing it down the
toilet). I had panic attacks that felt like heart attacks, but I was
unable to speak about the evilness that was my childhood. Saying
it would make it real, and I had struggled all my life to not think
about it. I had always known that I had been sexually abused. That
knowledge had never left me. But the enormity of that knowledge
and the constant pressure of having to maintain my silence had
created a legacy within my body. Headaches, irritable bowel, back
pain, gynaecological problems, an irrational fear of thunderstorms,
startle reaction, and sleeplessness were all clear indicators that
something was wrong.

But not one doctor ever asked me if I had ever been subjected to
sexual abuse as a child. My body was crying out, saying that something was wrong. But because no one asked me the question, I
knew, as the child had known, that it was not OK to talk about it.

Suicidal thoughts intruded once again and it felt like the only
recourse I had—to escape the constant barrage of flashbacks. My
life was a mess. I was off work sick. My husband could only look
on, helplessly, as I shrivelled up before him, into the posture of a
small child. I remember his hands hanging by his sides, unable to
reach out to me because I recoiled at the mere thought of a man's
hand touching my body. My father, though dead, was there. I could
see him, smell him, taste him. I gagged on the memory, it was so
real. It was real. I was in a parallel universe, twinned with the past
and present. Eventually I gained the courage I needed to disclose
my secret to my GP, which was a painful and shocking experience.
She sat motionless, and months later told me that she had felt helpless, aware that her knowledge about such abuse and the long-term
impact was inadequate.

Notwithstanding her lack of experience, we made our way together
down a pathway that could, so easily, have been the wrong one for
me. Given the state I was in, my GP could have had me admitted
to hospital—and it is likely that I would have gone down that
downward spiral of madness and the likelihood of misdiagnosis.
But, she had enough about her to realise that I might be suffering
something more readily identifiable as PTSD—and in doing so, she

started me on the pathway that saved my life. In 1994–1995 I was able to gain immediate access to trauma counselling through my employer. During sixteen sessions I worked in partnership with the psychotherapist to explore the memories that had so carefully been hidden (not all of them, though, for I am amnesic about large periods of my life prior to the age of ten). My psychotherapist worked gently with me and together we slowly unpeeled the onion-skin of memories. She tried several approaches with me before she found the one that worked best for me. The approach was eclectic and focused on the trauma but in a way that was humane and minimised triggering further trauma. My psychotherapist used different techniques as the need arose and was able to hear what I needed rather than imposing theoretical models that would have been unworkable for me. It was a partnership, and was important because it meant that an early foundation of trust was laid. Gradually I came to understand the link between my fear of thunderstorms [and] my childhood experiences. I understood why I had avoided certain environments and why intimacy of any kind (including friendship) was so difficult. My sexual relationship with my partner had taken a massive downward spiral—any touch evoked painful and intrusive memories. Initially I submitted to his sexual desires, because I felt guilty about saying "no". But in saying "yes", it only made it worse. The flashbacks intensified and I felt that life was no longer worth living. It had been impossible to believe that I could ever escape from the world that my life had become. I was able to find the will to live and my psychotherapist was instrumental in that, because she gave me the time to reflect on my experience and the feelings associated with it.

But for me, sanity came through meeting others who had endured a similar childhood (I met these survivors through the group CISters). It gave me an insight that my psychotherapist had never achieved into the full impact on my life that the abuse had made. I was a workaholic, obese, with no real friends—and the only good thing I had going for me was that I had a determination in my heart that my abuser was NOT going to win. Slowly I gained ground and as each new insight came I was able to see my symptoms diminish. The panic attacks tapered off, the intensity of the flashbacks dwindled, and my irritable bowel began to loosen some [of] its hold on me. I was able to breathe again. PTSD still walks beside me—the chronic impact of the abuse is not easily shaken off. At times of stress some of the symptoms return (such as startle reaction and insomnia)—but it is extremely rare for me to have flashbacks, which have only occurred twice in seven years. I saw my psycho-therapist again in 2001 for six sessions after a car accident and in 2003 for another six sessions after I was diagnosed with fibro-myalgia. It was helpful to see the same person because she knew my history and was able to connect the feelings of helplessness I felt on both of these occasions to my feelings about my childhood. But life is easier and simpler, and my returning good health brought with it a return to work and the opportunity for a new way of living: finally being able to relax after years of living on the edge of my nerves and looking over my shoulder. Anger was not an emotion I allowed myself as a child or as an adult. But anger is what I feel at times, and it is a powerful motivator and lifesaver. At times I wonder how my life would have been if someone had asked me decades ago whether I had ever been abused in my life. That question would have given me an opportunity to disclose my secret, and perhaps I would have gained a new quality of life, years earlier, rather than having to wait until I was nearly fifty. [Adapted, with the author's consent, from Royal College of Psychiatrists & The British Psychological Society, 2005]

Younger children who have experienced sexual abuse, violence, and neglect might or might not be referred for psychotherapeutic assessment or treatment.

The sexual abuse, violence, or neglect might not be known about, either because the child is too frightened to say or has no one that he or she trusts, or because he or she feels too ashamed, or the child may have pushed it out of his or her mind. If the child shows emotional or behaviour problems, these might be attributed to sexual abuse, violence, or neglect, or not.

The impact of sexual abuse, violence, or neglect on a child's and adolescent's development might be very obvious from the outset, or might only become apparent at key times in their life, such as puberty, adolescence, beginning of adult sexual relationships, motherhood and fatherhood, or bereavement.

Children, adolescents, or adults may seek psychotherapy because they wish to talk about their traumatic experiences. How-ever, some people might forget, or try to forget, their abusive expe-riences but find that their distress reveals itself in psychosomatic difficulties, but make no connection between their emotional or physical problems and their experiences of abuse.

Therapeutic help will need to be available when needed, during the course of the child's development into adulthood.

> Susanne was three when she was referred by Social Services for child psychotherapy after six months of sexual abuse by her mother's part- ner. She was now in the care of loving grandparents who were distressed by the level of her emotional disturbance. She was an angry and controlling little girl, who could not play at nursery and who would not sleep at night unless her grandmother followed an increas- ing number of rituals "to keep her safe". Over eighteen months [of] intensive three times a week psycho-analytic psychotherapy and sup- port for the grandparents, Susanne gradually recovered. Her anger covered up a tremendous sadness at losing her mother, her home, and a father figure who both spoiled her and scared her. She gradually gave up her sexualized behaviour as she discovered adults could love and care for her without exploiting her. She also began to play and learn, as her early trauma was worked through, and her internal emotional chaos resolved into understandable feelings. When she finished, she was a much warmer child, able to make friends, but her grandparents knew they may need to seek help for her if these early experiences were evoked again as she reached later stages of development.

Although not all victims will want or need or benefit from psychoanalytic psychotherapy, very many will need some form of talking therapy or other therapeutic or social support.

In circumstances when intensive psychoanalytic therapy is wanted and needed, victims often do not have the social or family support to enable them to engage most effectively with therapy, and to manage the feelings and memories that are stirred up as the therapy progresses.

Psychoanalytic treatments

Evidence

- People with a history of childhood trauma psychotherapy appear to respond more favourably to psychotherapy than medication.
- Evidence exists indicating that psychotherapy is superior to pharmacotherapy in the treatment of chronic depression in victims of childhood trauma.
- Highest quality evidence exists for the effectiveness of short-term dynamic psychotherapy in common mental disorders, and these benefits appear to be maintained in the long term.
- Evidence exists for the cost effectiveness of short-term dynamic psychotherapy in common mental disorders.
- Good quality evidence exists for the effectiveness of residential intensive dynamic psychotherapy and intensive outpatient dynamic psychotherapy in the treatment of personality disorders, and these benefits appear to be maintained or even increase in the long term.
- Intensive dynamic psychotherapy for personality disorders leads to considerable cost savings.

- Good quality evidence exists for the superiority of intensive dynamic psychotherapy over DBT in the treatment of severe personality disorder.
- There is evidence that the short-term benefits of CBT are not maintained in the long term.

Researching psychotherapy

Psychoanalytic clinicians tend to aim beyond simple reductions in symptom counts, towards more abstract, and harder to measure, goals such as resolution of conflict, insight, self-understanding, self-acceptance, personality change, integration, psychic maturity, etc. Historically, clinical psychodynamic research has emphasized the individual case study as a way of capturing the detail, nuanced richness, and uniqueness of each clinical case; this has been productive and led to an outpouring of understanding and clinical theories of the development and function of different states of mind. There has rightly been concern that an emphasis on quantification would obliterate the very detail that is necessary to come to an understanding of abnormal states of mind (Fonagy, 2002).

None the less, psychodynamic investigators have also long used quantitative methods to great effect. See, for example, the pioneering researches of psychoanalysts into the emotional and health effects of the hospitalization of infants, which has led to profound changes in the way that young children are cared for in institutions (Spitz, 1945), on the effects of maternal deprivation and maternal depression on the developing infant's mind (Bowlby, 1967, 1973, 1980), and on attachment measurement and classification (Ainsworth, Blehar, Waters, & Wall, 1978). Contemporary research on mentalization and affect regulation (Fonagy, Gergely, Jurist, & Target, 2004) has combined insights from psychoanalysis with modern neuroscience in an elaboration of how human genes and brain have evolved in such a way that the full development of the individual child's brain and mind is only possible through close emotional interactions between the child and its parents from the start of life (Schore, 2003; Solms & Turnbull, 2002; Wilkinson, in press).

Currently, in England and Wales, decisions on funding or commissioning services rely heavily on guidelines produced by the National Institute for Health and Clinical Excellence (NICE); however, these have been criticized for their selective review of the literature and also their over-reliance on meta-analyses of randomized controlled trials (Smith, 2007).

The randomized controlled trial design is a powerful tool for looking at certain types of health care intervention, especially for assessing certain medical treatments—taking some types of pills, for example—where participants can be given either the medicine under investigation, a comparison treatment or placebo and not know which treatment it is that they are receiving. If participants cannot be blinded to the treatment that they are taking, for example in psychotherapy, then the participants' preferences and expectations will affect their response to the treatment. Randomized controlled trials and meta-analyses can also be effective ways of minimizing biases in experimental design.

However, an exclusive reliance on meta-analyses and randomized controlled trials in psychotherapy research represents a misunderstanding of the strengths of meta-analyses and randomized controlled trials, and of their limitations. It is misguided to believe that everything can be investigated equally well in a randomized control trial.

Randomized trials can be inappropriate for a number of reasons: it may be impractical to have sufficiently large groups to examine the differences between different treatments, or because the required follow-up period is too long, or because the very act of randomization may reduce the effectiveness of the intervention because the treatment requires the participants' active participation, which in turn depends on their beliefs and preferences (Brewin & Bradley, 1989). The particular participants might be unwilling to be randomized, or to submit to repeated lengthy follow-up assessments.

There are detailed reviews of the place of randomized controlled trials in health care research and their limitations (Black, 1996), and of the methodological, practical, ethical, and theoretical obstacles in applying randomized controlled trial methodology to psychodynamic psychotherapy (Fonagy, 2002; Roth & Fonagy, 2005).

Children who have been sexually or
physically abused or neglected

A recent critical review of the research literature on the psychological treatment of child and adolescent psychiatric disorders emphasizes the many ethical and practical problems that researchers face in this field. Clinicians attempting to implement research evidence are rarely treating children with a clear-cut psychiatric disorder within a supportive family. Indeed, the long-term outcome of childhood disorders is not only a function of the child's disorder, but also of their family and social background. This can limit the applicability of outcome research for clinical services (Target & Fonagy, 2005).

The review concludes that, in many respects, the field of outcome research in children and adolescents is at too early a stage to make many recommendations about which treatments show most benefit for which disorders.

An earlier review of the research literature on the treatment of children who have experienced sexual abuse emphasizes that child sexual abuse is not a condition, but an experience linked to a wide range of other adverse experiences, and the children often have multiple problems, including an extremely wide range of psychiatric difficulties, or apparently no disturbance at all. The authors conclude that a range of psychotherapeutic modalities is required, that short-term symptom-driven packages of care will not help all children, that services need to have a long-term orientation, that some children will need long-term psychotherapy, and that services need to be more clearly orientated to the children's needs (Ramchandani & Jones, 2003).

In one of the few randomized studies of psychoanalytic psychotherapy for sexually abused children, seventy-five sexually abused girls (aged 6–14 years) were randomized to receive either combined psychotherapeutic and psycho-educational group therapy complemented by supportive work with the carers, or individual psychoanalytic psychotherapy complemented by supportive work with carers. The sample was severely affected, with over 30% exposed to multiple perpetrators. Both types of therapy were associated with reductions in depression and anxiety and an improvement in overall functioning. However, there was a clinically and statistically significant difference between the groups with regard to post traumatic stress disorder symptoms (re-experiencing of traumatic events and persistent avoidance of stimuli) in favour of individual psychoanalytic psychotherapy (Trowell et al., 2002). It is argued that this is important, since post traumatic stress disorder has potential to become chronic. In addition, the authors note that, despite the overall shift towards improvement over time with treatment, a small number of girls became more symptomatic with the passage of time and treatment. They suggest that these girls might have been using dissociation to cut themselves off from their traumatic experiences, but with therapy they were able to start to process their experiences; however, the short-term therapy was insufficient and they would require longer-term therapy.

The vast majority of children who receive treatment following abuse do so in local Child and Adolescent Mental Health Services. However, clinical experience reveals that often the most traumatized children are alienated from their families or are in care and cannot be sufficiently helped by outpatient services. Such children require safety and emotional security. Very disturbed children may exceed the capacities of their carers, schools, and outpatient Child and Adolescent Mental Health Services to provide safety and security. These children may require specialist residential therapeutic settings.

Adults who have been sexually or physically
abused or neglected in childhood

Few studies have looked at how childhood sexual or physical violence or neglect may influence responses to treatment with medication or psychotherapy for common mental disorders. This could be because childhood sexual and physical abuse and neglect have such a wide range of outcomes. Randomized controlled trials work best when the participants are similar and the groups are homogeneous. If groups are heterogeneous (i.e., contain individuals who vary with different symptoms or disorders) then larger sample sizes are required, otherwise the differences within the groups will obscure the differences between the treatments, and significant differences between treatments will not be detected. A randomized controlled trial of people who had experienced child-hood sexual abuse or neglect would have very heterogeneous groups; this would require prohibitively large samples and might still not produce useful results. Reflecting this, most clinical research on psychotherapeutic and pharmacological treatment chooses samples on the basis of diagnosis in order to minimize heterogeneity within samples. The standard critical review of psychotherapy treatment research analyses trials by diagnosis, and not by the presence of factors such as childhood sexual or physical abuse or neglect (Roth & Fonagy, 2005).

One study looked at the response of people with chronic depression to drug treatment and to psychotherapy, and looked for differences between those who had a history of childhood trauma (loss, sexual or physical violence, or neglect) and those who did not. In this study, patients were randomized to receive either antidepressant medication or the cognitive–behavioural analysis system of psychotherapy. This is a structured, time-limited psychotherapy, developed to treat depression, which uses elements from cognitive–behavioural therapy *and* interpersonal therapy. Most similar studies of the treatment of depression find that medication has a similar effect to psychotherapy of whatever type. However, in this study, the results were striking: among those with a history of childhood trauma (loss, sexual or physical violence, or neglect) psychotherapy alone was superior to antidepressant medication alone. Furthermore, the combination of psychotherapy and drug treatment was only marginally superior to psychotherapy alone among those with a history of childhood abuse (Nemeroff et al., 2003).

Although this research needs to be replicated, it suggests that people with a history of childhood trauma may benefit more from psychotherapy, and benefit less from medication, than those without such a history. Furthermore, this suggests that treatment trials that do not distinguish between participants with experiences of early trauma might be misleading. Future trials of psychiatric treatments should consider early trauma as an important potential confounding factor.

The evidence for psychoanalytic psychotherapies in various psychiatric conditions, with or without a history of childhood sexual or physical abuse or neglect, is discussed below.

Evidence for psychoanalytic psychotherapies

Despite the obstacles to, and limitations of, randomized controlled trials described above, there is now a wide and rich evidence base for the use of psychodynamic psychotherapies, long and short term, in a wide range of conditions. A recent Cochrane meta-analysis of twenty-three RCTs of short-term psychodynamic psychotherapy found it to have modest to moderate effects relative to controls across a broad range of common mental disorders (Abbass, Hancock, Henderson, & Kisely, 2006). In somatic, depressive, and general symptoms, treatment effects were increased over long-term follow-up, suggesting maintained or increased gains in the long term. Benefits were observed across depression, anxiety, somatic, and general measures, as well as social adjustment. Individual studies also found improvements in interpersonal relationships, reduced self-injury, and weight gain in anorexia nervosa, suggesting behavioural as well as symptomatic gains. Moreover, the observed reduction in somatic symptoms contributed to observed reductions in healthcare use and improved occupational functioning. Indeed, there may be financial benefit to these systems through providing this brief treatment. A further review of the cost effectiveness studies found that treatment costs had been recouped within three years (Abbass, 2003).

It would be a mistake to assume that psychotherapy, when it does not lead to an improvement, is merely ineffective. Current research suggests that patients with a weaker sense of their own subjectivity, such as those who have received a diagnosis of borderline personality disorder, find it harder to compare the validity of their own perceptions of the way their mind works with the explanations and models that a "mind expert" (clinician) offers. Both cognitively based and dynamically orientated therapies can give ready-made answers and provide illusory stability by inducing a process of pseudo-mentalization in which the patient takes on the explanations without question and makes them his/her own. Conversely, both types of perspective can be summarily and angrily dismissed as overly simplistic and patronizing, which in turn fuels a sense of abandonment, and feelings of isolation and desperation (Fonagy & Bateman, 2006).

Severe personality disorders are commonly associated with histories of early abuse and attachment difficulties. The evidence base for the treatment of severe personality disorders has been transformed in the last decade. There are now high quality controlled and randomized controlled trials that indicate the effectiveness of inpatient psychodynamic therapeutic community treatment, step down treatment (combined inpatient treatment followed by outpatient treatment) and day hospital or partial hospitalization treatment in treating severe personality and neurotic disorders (Bateman & Fonagy, 1999; Chiesa, Fonagy, Holmes, & Drahorad, 2004; Chiesa, Fonagy, Holmes, Drahorad, & Harrison-Hall, 2002).

These psychodynamic treatments have been demonstrated to be superior to dialectical behaviour therapy and supportive psychotherapy (Clarkin, Levy, Lenzenweger, & Kernberg, 2007). Furthermore these treatment programmes have been demonstrated to lead to substantial cost savings after treatment (Bateman & Fonagy, 2003; Beecham, Sleed, Knapp, Chiesa, & Drahorad, 2006).

Cassel Hospital

The Cassel Hospital is an NHS national specialist service for the assessment and treatment of adults, young people and families with intractable personality and family problems. 42% of a sample of Cassel patients reported sexual abuse by the age of 10 years (Chiesa, Fonagy, Holmes, Drahorad, & Harrison-Hall, 2002), other adverse experiences include physical abuse, neglect, parental mental ill health, being in care. Patients are usually diagnosed with severe personality disorders and have histories of abusing themselves or are considered to be a risk to their own children.

The Cassel Hospital offers a treatment that includes individual psychoanalytic psychotherapy, group therapy, therapeutic community living and psychosocial nursing. It is an effective treatment for people who have exhausted other avenues of help from mental health, children's and social care services.

This is in contrast to recent government-sponsored research into the long-term effects of cognitive behavioural therapy (CBT), which found that the positive effects of CBT identified in the original trials were eroded over longer time periods. No evidence was found for an association between more intensive therapy and more enduring effects of CBT. The cost-effectiveness analysis showed no advantages of CBT over non-CBT. Patients with PTSD did particularly poorly; there was a 40% real increase in healthcare costs over the follow-up period, mainly due to an increase in prescribing (Durham et al., 2005).

Surveys of users of Mental Health services consistently find that patients want more access to psychological therapies (Mind, 2002). It is government policy that patients should be offered a range of effective treatment options that they can choose between (Department of Health, 2004).

Stepped care

The currently favoured model of organizing the delivery of psychotherapies to minimize cost and maximize coverage is that of stepped care. Emerging findings from VVAPP research also support a stepped care approach, as set out in the *Improving Access to Psychological Therapies Guide: Commissioning a Brighter Future* (Department of Health, 2007), the NICE stepped care model, and the Royal College of Paediatrics and Child Health guidance on mapping pathways and implementing networks.

In a stepped care model, treatments are ranked in a hierarchy with the least restrictive (in practical terms this means the least expensive) treatments offered before more expensive ones. If patients fail to respond to this they are then offered progressively more expensive treatments. In reality, a stepped care model might not be quite so restrictive and patients may well be offered a restricted range of treatments at each step of the protocol. Stepped care models have some theoretical attractions; potentially they might ensure that:

• the most expensive and intensive treatments are only given to those patients who have not benefited from less expensive treatments;
• patients will only receive as much treatment as they need and not have their time wasted by enrolling in lengthy and restrictive treatments when they might have benefited from shorter treatments;

- by using resources more efficiently, more people can receive treatment from the same resources.

However, the stepped care model makes several assumptions that have not been tested and also has the potential to have negative effects, such as:

- wasting resources by offering patients treatments that they do not want;
- wasting resources by offering patients treatments that are unlikely to benefit them;
- giving patients treatments that may be harmful to them;
- alienating patients by wasting their time and obliging them to "go through the motions" before they can get access to the treatments that they want or believe will help them. This is particularly relevant for those who may get held up at the initial stage, which is relevant for non-traumatized minor depression, and decide never to attempt psychological treatment of any sort ever again at the more intensive higher steps appropriate for them;
- wasting opportunities to build strong therapeutic alliances by not offering them effective treatments that they are motivated to receive when they need them, and thus discouraging them from making a good alliance with an alternative treatment source.

In *Commissioning a Brighter Future*, the NHS has set out its aspiration to ensure that the right number of people are offered a choice of the right services at the right time with the right results.

However, the right treatment can only be offered if a good enough assessment has been made. In the absence of an expert assessment, there is a risk that inadequately trained generic practitioners using standardized screening tools could wrongly diagnose asymptomatic individuals as coping well, when really the assessment has missed significant difficulties with attachment and coping style. This can lead to people with abusive experience being stuck at step one of the depression stepped care programme, when their histories of trauma, abuse, or dissociative symptoms suggest that the stepped care for depression is unlikely to benefit them and may be harmful (Bower & Gilbody, 2005).

In order to minimize these possible negative effects, we propose that a modification be incorporated into the existing NICE stepped care model that might be seen as a form of stepped assessment.

Professionals at the point of initial assessment, usually in primary care, who might not have experience or confidence in the assessment of individuals who have experienced significant childhood trauma, would be trained to ask additional screening questions to identify dissociative symptoms: derealization, depersonalization, fugue states or flashbacks, and also whether the patient had had traumatic or sexually abusive experiences.

Routine exploration of violence and abuse in specialist mental health settings is already Department of Health national policy (Department of Health, 2003). A number of mental health trusts are currently piloting implementation of this as part of the Mental Health Trusts Collaboration Project (National Institute for Mental Health in England [NIMHE]). Following attendance at a training day, staff of all disciplines are encouraged to incorporate the following direct question in their routine assessments of patients: "Have you ever experienced any physical, sexual, or emotional abuse, at any time in your life?"

Suggested questions to be incorporated into the initial assessment for stepped care could be:

1. Questions to screen for dissociative experiences:
    (a) "Have you ever felt as if you were outside your own body, perhaps looking down on yourself from the ceiling or from a corner of the room?" If yes, "How often?"
    (b) "Do you ever find yourself with a blank in your mind as to what has been happening for the last minute or so?" If yes, "How often?"
    (c) "Have you ever lost your memory for a period of several hours?"
    (d) "Do you ever get flashbacks—that is consistently recurring memories of something upsetting that has happened to you, memories that keep coming back over and over again?" If yes, "How often?"

2. Questions to screen for a history of abuse or trauma:
    Either the direct approach advocated by the Mental Health Trusts Collaboration Project: "Have you ever experienced any

physical, sexual, or emotional abuse, at any time in your life?",
or a more tentative approach such as: "We have to ask this
of everyone to work out what step to take next, so I wonder
if anything ever happened to you earlier in life that could
be described as traumatic. Something like being attacked or
beaten or badly taken care of? You don't necessarily have to
tell me what it was (though of course you can if you want).
Just whether something happened or not." PAUSE. "Perhaps
being sexually approached against your will? Something like
that?"

If the individual responds yes to a history of abuse or trauma,
or to the screening questions for dissociation (1(c) has happened or
the experiences in 1(a), (b), and (d) are happening fairly frequently)
they should proceed to a more detailed assessment of their attachment and coping style rather than staying at step one of the NICE
guidelines depression programme.

Graduate mental health workers working in the stepped care
system for depression, for example, would be able to ask such
screening questions. Tools already exist for this purpose that have
been used in this way (Brown, Craig, Harris, Handley, & Harvey,
2007a,b,c).

If the results of this initial screening for trauma or abuse were
positive, and answers to these screening questions suggested some
form of dissociative symptoms, patients would be referred for a further, more detailed, assessment by a clinician with more specialized
training.

Detailed assessments of patients with trauma, abuse, or dissociative symptoms typically take three or four sessions.

This model of detailed assessments, or three or four sessions,
has been in use by the Women's Therapy Centre for some years. In
addition to providing adequate assessment of people with complex histories and symptoms, detailed assessments also have therapeutic function, providing some psychotherapeutic holding while
individuals are waiting for psychotherapy treatment to start.

Investing more time in the assessment stage of stepped services
has potential to use resources more appropriately and economically.
Such stepped assessments should be piloted. The proposed system
might involve the following steps.

1. Recognition and identification in primary and other health care settings by workers with level 1 training—initial assessment.
2. Further assessment and diagnosis by expert assessors—of mental health problems and underlying causes of abuse/violence.
3. Bibliotherapy and guided self help—the NICE *Guidelines on Self-Harm* (2004 noted the wealth of survivor literature for, and often by, victims of violence and sexual abuse.
4. Practical advice and support services and information from independent and voluntary sector organizations, advocacy by Independent Domestic Violence and Sexual Violence Advisers.
5. Telephone support—Women's Aid and Refuge run a national helpline and online bookings for refuge places, and over one hundred of The Survivors Trust and rape crisis organizations provide telephone help lines.
6. Group therapy.
7. Specialist services (black and minority ethnic groups, physical and learning disabilities, GLBT, trafficking, sexual exploitation, self-harm).
8. The full range of long-term one-to-one talking therapies—counselling, CBT, psychoanalytic psychotherapies, psychoanalysis, other psychotherapies.

Not everyone who has experienced childhood abuse, violence, or neglect will have the same need or wish for psychotherapeutic interventions. But many will need some sort of psychotherapy, some short term, and some will need long-term intensive psychoanalytic psychotherapy.

Different people will need different psychotherapeutic approaches, and the same individual might need different interventions over time. An understanding of integration as a gradual process lends itself to a modular approach with periods of treatment delivered at key points in the patient's life experience.

To deliver effective stepped care, Primary Care Trusts and Local Authorities must commission the appropriate range of psychotherapies and other therapeutic interventions across sectors.

These services need to be sufficient in number and available to people at the right times in their lives.

The process of psychoanalytic psychotherapy

Trauma covers a continuum of experience that might bring people to psychotherapy. What matters most in the consulting-room is not so much what was done to the child, but what it did to the child, how the child was affected, what the child then made of it, and how that has affected the child or adult who presents for treatment. Patterns of insecure and disorganized attachment tend to be stable. Dissociated aspects of the personality and repressed memories of experiences of abuse can persist, unmodified, out of conscious awareness.

Deep-seated trauma requires sustained treatment in depth over time to effect change. Insecure or disorganized attachment, dissociated aspects of the self, and repressed memories of abuse can be overcome if the patient is able to develop and experience a secure attachment in his or her life. An integrated personality is a hard-won developmental achievement for the person who has experienced severe traumatization. For some, this will only happen in a psychotherapeutic relationship.

The therapist's task is to help the patient to build a secure trusting relationship with the therapist. Understanding and working through the obstacles to the building of a secure trusting relationship is at the core of the treatment. This must begin with the therapist giving the patient the experience of having their accounts of the abuse accepted, something that they may never have had before.

Affect regulation

The initial development of mind is dependent on each individual's early experience of relating to others and arises from intimate interactions with the mother and the father. Maturation of the orbitofrontal cortex is experience dependent and is expressed in the growth and stabilization of its dense interconnections with both cortical and subcortical areas (Schore, 1994). Affectively focused treatment alters the frontal lobes of the brain in a way that is detectable by functional imaging studies (Solms & Turnbull, 2002).

The building blocks that go to establish attachment to carers in the beginning of life are activated again in the psychotherapeutic relationship that develops in the consulting-room. The inferior colliculus is a nucleus in the auditory pathway between the ear and higher centres of the brain. It also mediates affective process, and is described as the region where "our mother's voice may leave forever its first affective imprint". This might explain why sound is so effective at synchronizing and regulating emotions (Panskepp & Bernatzky, 2002), and also why the prosodic aspects of the psycho-therapist's voice become so important to the patient with early relational trauma who is seeking to learn a new kind of attachment (Williams, 2004).

Lengthy silences in psychotherapy may be unbearable to those patients who have experienced early relational abuse. There is a need for caution in the use of silence with these patients; silence is ambiguous, and activates implicit memories of abuse and high levels of fear and anxiety (Bollas, 1987; Chu, 1998; Cozolino, 2002).

It may be premature to speculate on precisely how psycho-therapy leads to development in the brain. In general terms, it is possible to say that psychotherapy extends the inhibitory influence of the prefrontal cortices over the emotional and impulsive limbic structures. This much has been demonstrated by functional neuro-imaging. Furthermore, it appears that this takes place via the inter-nalization of the therapist's voice, which leads to an increase in the capacity for reflection on the internal emotional state (Solms & Turnbull, 2002).

The first phase of treatment is the establishment of the thera-peutic attachment in the context of a secure therapeutic frame. This permits stabilization, and symptom reduction begins. Fear of trauma-derived mental actions, of dissociated parts of the person-ality, and of attachment and attachment loss are worked with at this stage.

The second phase of treatment involves carefully paced explo-ration of traumatic memories, with particular attention to the regu-lation of states of hyper- and hypo-arousal. It is during this phase that experiences and feelings can be given names, and thought about.

The final phase of treatment is that of personality integration and rehabilitation. As the patient attempts to come to terms with his or her past, there inevitably arise painful experiences of grief as well as the struggle to engage with the world in a different way. It has been said that "overcoming the phobia of intimacy is perhaps the pinnacle of successful treatment" (van der Hart, Nijenhuis, & Steele, 2006).

A staged approach to individual sessions is important for patients with trauma histories. The initial period in the room allows for the patient to settle back into the room and into the continued exploration of the relationship with the therapist. The middle part of the session will be the safest part of the session for the patient to engage with the more painful aspects of early experience re-experienced in the transference relationship. For such patients the last part of the session needs to be devoted to recovery, so that the patient may leave in a safe state.

The therapist's aim is neither reassurance, nor avoidance of the trauma, but rather to address the point of pain while enabling the patient to stay "in mind" and able to think and reflect. To this end, the therapist should avoid sustained states of over or under arousal in the patient.

In the consulting-room, frequent states of hyper-arousal and the emergence of flashbacks overwhelm the patient's capacity to think and reflect on their emotional state. Affect regulation is central to any such therapy.

Various techniques have evolved to help counteract over-arousal: a lowering of tone and slowing of speech, or it may be possible to help the patient to modify their experience by use of a simple phrase such as "that was then, not now". This process of cure is not initially that of making the unconscious conscious, as with interpretation, rather it is the interactive experience within the therapeutic relationship that enables affect regulation.

Patient–therapist interaction

As psychotherapy progresses, both psychotherapist and patient will be affected by their current attachment experiences and by changes that occur through stress, loss, or good experience. Part of the task of the psychotherapist will be to use the transference experience to help the patient to explore and become aware of their early attachment relationships and able to look at the way this may be mirrored in their current relationships. This focus on attachment

relationships and their related affects can change enduring attachment styles and derived ways of relating, feeling, and behaving,
and lead to a changed experience of attachment, characterized as
learned secure (Wilkinson, 2006).

Both psychotherapist and patient have a series of attachment
experiences, past and current, that contribute to the attachment
style that they bring to the therapeutic attachment. In the case of the
patient, it might well be an avoidant style learned early, or might
be anxious or perhaps disorganized. The analyst might have been
fortunate enough to start with a secure attachment, or might well
have done a great deal of work in his or her own analysis to move
from one of the other styles to "learned secure".

Modification of technique

Psychoanalytic approaches can be adapted to working with diverse
groups of individuals.

Individuals with severe and complex post traumatic stress
disorder may avoid talking about their symptoms from a fear that
they are going mad. The intensity of their flashbacks may be such
that they dissociate and become lost in the horrors of their past
experiences. The Traumatic Stress Service at the Maudsley Hospital
offers patients individual and group psychoanalytic psychotherapy
that is adapted to addressing these overwhelming feelings (de
Zulueta, 2006; Lab, Santos, & de Zulueta, 2008). Adaptations
include the following.

- Psycho-education to give an explanation or "cognitive blue-
  print" of how post traumatic stress disorder, flashbacks, and
  dissociation occur, and why it is important to focus on the past
  experiences.
- Relaxation techniques using audio tapes, guided imagery, and
  the creation of safe places are taught to counteract the feelings
  of helplessness associated with traumatic experiences.
- To prevent the patient becoming dissociated and lost in the
  horrors of their past, the psychotherapist may keep in verbal
  contact with the patient by commenting on what he or she sees
  or hears and reminding the patient that the event was in the

past. Patients can be further helped to retain contact with the present through various grounding techniques, such as maintaining eye contact, holding on to something, and, most importantly, by both becoming aware of, and working through with the psychotherapist, the feelings of shame.

- If the psychotherapy fails to progress, then eye movement desensitization and reprocessing (EMDR) may be added and the psychotherapist may accompany the patient to the EMDR sessions, so that the memories and experiences that come up during EMDR can be integrated into the psychotherapy sessions.
- A specialized, ten-month-long group is offered to survivors of child sexual abuse, which addresses and reduces their levels of dissociation through combined psychoanalytic, cognitive, and systemic approaches (Ney & Peters, 1995).

Psychoanalytic understanding and attachment theory also provide a theoretical underpinning to the work of therapeutic communities and other attachment based therapeutic organizations and programmes such as Integrated Systemic Therapy, as provided by Childhood First (previously known as Peper Harow), and Kids' Company (see "Socially excluded children", above) (Blunden & Carter, 2007; Kennedy, Heymans, & Tischler, 1987; Main, 1981; Warren & Dolan, 2001).

Patients in psychoanalytic psychotherapy and psychoanalysis who have experienced incestuous abuse might find silences particularly discomforting, interpretations might be experienced as intrusive, and exploration of the patients' thoughts and fantasies might be felt to be seductive. The patient might reveal contempt for their own feelings and thoughts. The psychoanalytic psychotherapist might need to help the patient to put these experiences into words as soon as possible to avoid the patient being overwhelmed with claustrophobic anxiety and panic (Bollas, 1987).

Assessment

- One of the most important contributions of psychoanalysis has been its developmental model of personality and psycho-

pathology, and its use of the exploration of these as a therapeutic activity.

- Aetiological research exploring such developmental models has
revealed the diverse outcomes and differing pathways from
childhood neglect and abuse to painful adult experience.
- People who have suffered abuse or neglect follow different
developmental pathways. The first step in psychoanalytical
psychotherapy is a proper assessment of which particular pathway has been theirs. Which style of defence have they been able
to use to cope with the trauma?
- Different behaviours and coping or defence styles require
different responses in psychotherapy.
- The apparent absence of psychiatric symptoms or obviously
abnormal behaviour might mask serious disturbance in psychic
function with very abnormal defensive style and attachment
disorganization.

Assessment of children, adolescents, and adults in psychoanalytic psychotherapy serves a number of functions. In common with
any psychiatric assessment there is an assessment of any symptom
pattern or psychiatric disorder that might exist, and an assessment
of any underlying or predisposing personality pattern or disorder.

In addition, there is an assessment of coping style, or defensive
functioning, and an assessment of attachment relationships in the
past and present. These should indicate where the patient's current
emotional conflicts lie, and why this person is unable to get the
support and caring that they need from their close family and
friends. The attachment style will also influence the development of
the psychotherapeutic relationship.

Finally, there is an assessment of the individual's ability to put
their feelings into words and to respond to the psychotherapist's
interventions, sometimes referred to as psychological minded-
ness, which will have some implication for the patient's ability to
engage with the psychotherapist and use the psychotherapy (Mace,
1995).

The length of the assessment is variable. Typically, between two
and five sessions may be required to clarify the patient's difficulties
and what form of psychotherapy may be of most help to them. The
form of the assessment will vary according to the institutional

setting, the type(s) of psychotherapy available, and if the assessor will also be the psychotherapist.

In assessing children and adolescents, close attention has to be paid to their level of emotional development and the relationships and emotional environment within the family.

As discussed when considering children and adults with disability, the difficulties of dependent patients have to be considered in relation to the dynamics of the family or institution in which they live. Will the family or institution be able to support the patient if psychotherapy starts, or will this introduce further difficulties for the patient?

Not all people with a history of childhood sexual or physical abuse or neglect seeking psychotherapeutic help want or need long-term psychotherapy. However, it is important in these circumstances to have a detailed assessment of their difficulties, strengths, and weaknesses, in order to avoid offering inappropriate or potentially harmful treatments.

As described above in *stepped care*, a screening assessment for childhood sexual or physical abuse, neglect, or dissociative symptoms, may usefully be built into a stepped care protocol to identify individuals in need of an in-depth psychotherapeutic assessment.

Safety

Many health service units or therapy organizations will not take on patients who are in a situation where abuse is ongoing. Their primary requisite is "safety first", and then start treatment.

Unfortunately, this denies the possibility of psychotherapy to precisely the most vulnerable, those that have been unable to escape from their abusers. Inevitably, there are conflicting pressures. The person might need psychotherapeutic work in order to be able to cope with the challenges of changing their situation.

There is a consensus that complex trauma-related disorders are most appropriately treated with a phase- or stage-orientated approach. The most common structure for this is a treatment consisting of three phases or stages: achieving safety, after which stabilization of symptoms can occur, and only then can symptom reduction take place.

Training

Working with sexually abused children and adults is extremely challenging. In-depth therapeutic work with severely traumatized and distressed children or adults, such as those who have been sexually abused, needs experienced and qualified practitioners.

Insufficiently trained mental health workers should not be asked to take on work that is beyond their level of skill and training without access to appropriate consultation, supervision, and training by suitably qualified and experienced psychodynamic psychotherapists.

As sufficient trained professionals are not available in some areas, there should be an expectation that consultation and training for child-care and mental health professionals who wish to develop these skills are made available in every region by trained psychodynamic psychotherapists. Such assistance may also be available from within the specialist voluntary sector from agencies supporting victims of sexual abuse.

It is essential to require a minimum standard of expertise. The expectation must remain that severely sexually abused children and adults should be treated by suitably qualified psychotherapists, otherwise they will not receive the help that they need, or might indeed be further harmed. In addition, the professionals will be at increased risk of burnout and committing mistakes.

Psychoanalytic psychotherapist training

Psychoanalytic psychotherapy requires of its practitioners a thorough understanding of the ups and downs of their own psychological development, in order to understand sensitively those of another person.

Careful evaluation for training is necessary, with the core of the training being personal psychoanalytic therapy or analysis by appropriately experienced therapists. In addition, the training consists of careful supervision of clinical work by recognized supervisors as well as an understanding of theoretical concepts.

Psychoanalytic psychotherapists may train with a number of organizations.

The British Psychoanalytic Council (www.psychoanalytic-council. org) is a voluntary regulator for a number of psychoanalytic member organizations that provide training in psychoanalysis, analytical psychology, psychoanalytic psychotherapy, or child psychotherapy.

Each training organization has its own requirements for training, but most require applicants to have a degree or qualification in the field of medicine, psychology, or social work (or equivalent) and some experience in the field of mental health.

All of the BPC trainings are for a minimum of four years and require candidates to undertake personal analysis or therapy with an approved psychoanalyst or psychotherapist at least three times a week for the duration of the training. Candidates are also required to have extensive supervised clinical experience with two approved supervisors and to attend seminars covering theory and technique.

The United Kingdom Council for Psychotherapy (www. psychotherapy.org.uk) is another voluntary regulator and umbrella organization for a range of therapy training organizations; it has sections for Psychoanalytic and Psychodynamic Psychotherapy, and Psychoanalytically based Therapy with Children, among other modalities.

Medical psychotherapists (psychiatrists in psychotherapy) are registered with the General Medical Council (www.gmc-uk.org), and, if appropriate, might also be registered with the BPC or UKCP.

Training for child psychotherapy

The Association of Child Psychotherapists (www.acp.uk.net) is the professional organization for child psychotherapy in the UK. It recognizes and monitors five training programmes in child and adolescent psychotherapy. Trainees must have experience of long-term (up to two years), intensive (three to five times per week) psychotherapy with children and adolescents of different ages, plus a range of experience with less intensive psychotherapies and child-focused work with parents. Personal psychoanalysis is required at least four times a week throughout the four-year training.

Supervision

There is no doubt that secondary or vicarious traumatization is a very dangerous aspect of working with people who have experienced abuse or neglect in childhood. Burnout can easily happen; the traumatic memories and feelings of patients can lodge inside the professional and have an impact on their work and home lives (Morrison, 2007).

Supervision is a mechanism for the protection of the patient and the psychotherapist. Psychotherapy is an emotionally intense activity that makes many demands on the psychotherapist and the patient. They both want the psychotherapy to open up new avenues for the individual, but often psychotherapy can be very painful and the patient can bring complex needs to the psychotherapist. For instance, patients might feel discouraged or impatient. They might fault their psychotherapists for not being able to make them institute the changes they want faster. Patients might bring vestiges of abusive relationships that they have previously experienced to the psychotherapeutic relationship itself and anticipate that psychotherapists will be cruel and exploitative in the ways that they have experienced in previous relationships.

Supervision enables psychotherapists to carefully reflect on such issues so that they do not unwittingly get boxed into positions where they are unable to help.

The material that a patient might bring to psychotherapy can be extremely distressing. Even with appropriate professional training, the specific conundrums that a patient experiences are disturbing. That disturbance is brought into the psychotherapeutic relationship and, for example, can incline psychotherapists to want patients to be more forthright in their own defence of themselves. Or patients' intense anxiety, linked with wishes to change, might encourage psychotherapists to think that patients are more able than they actually are to find a different response to the situations that they encounter.

The supervision can provide a third ear to psychotherapists' concerns. It can enable psychotherapists to help patients tolerate their own anxieties or difficulties and sit and take time to explore different possible responses, and thus come to considered, measured, and judicious responses for themselves. Psychotherapy is not about pushing patients to act, but enabling them to find responses that are not impulsive, automatic, or immediately reactive, but more considered and measured. In this way, psychotherapy can help to build new capacities in hurt and damaged individuals.

Much of the material a psychotherapist hears can be violent and shame inducing for the psychotherapist and patient. Psychotherapists need professional support to acknowledge the impact of the patients' material on themselves so that they can absorb and then digest—outside of the psychotherapy sessions—their own personal reactions. In this way, psychotherapists can provide empathy without overly identifying with the patient.

Sometimes the specifics of patients' experiences can resonate with issues from psychotherapists' own lives. This can be helpful in creating bonds with patients. But, if the specifics touch painful issues that have occurred in psychotherapists' own backgrounds, then the psychotherapists may need to reflect on the emotional residues from their own personal experiences so that they make appropriate responses to their patients.

The aim in supervision is to point the way forward so that psychotherapists can be both compassionate and yet separate out their own history from the accounts of the patients; thus, psychotherapists are always acting in the patients' best interests.

The need for adequate psychotherapeutic supervision for clinicians working with the sexually abused cannot be replaced by case and time management supervision.

Services

Sexual assault referral centres (SARCs)

Sexual Assault Referral Centres are one-stop locations where female and male victims of rape and serious sexual assault can receive medical care and counselling, and have the opportunity to assist the police investigation, including undergoing a forensic examination.

Most SARCs are joint ventures between the police and Primary Care Trusts, with close involvement of the voluntary sector.

SARCs are an important in delivering enhanced care to victims of recent rape and serious sexual assault, but they are not designed to offer long-term support and do not normally provide services for victims of historic sexual violence.

In the short term, SARCs offer crisis workers to give support and counselling if wanted. There is recognition of the need for follow-up services, including psychosocial support and talking therapies (Department of Health, Children and Mental Health Division and Home Office, 2005).

Independent and voluntary sectors

The specialist voluntary sector has, over the past thirty years, developed creative and effective ways of working with survivors, based on a range of psychotherapeutic models and care and support packages that clients have made an active choice to access, and outcomes evidenced through service outcomes and direct feedback from survivors and therapists.

Examples of independent, voluntary, and survivor organizations

The Survivors' Trust

> The Survivors' Trust has a membership base of 125 individual agencies, specialist voluntary sector services providing mental health services, emotional and practical support, counselling and advice for men, women and children who are victims of rape, sexual violence and childhood sexual abuse, their partners, families and supporters.
>
> The Survivors' Trust membership includes 100 agencies working with adult survivors and child victims of childhood sexual abuse and 91 agencies providing services for victims of rape. 77 agencies provide crisis intervention services, including help lines and Independent Sexual Violence Adviser services. The Survivors' Trust membership also includes Sexual Assault Referral Centres based in Wales and Portsmouth.
>
> Specialist sexual violence and abuse services together with children's charities have developed a holistic, needs led approach to service provision for vulnerable groups of victims and survivors with complex needs, based on over 30 years' experience of direct service delivery. [The Survivors' Trust: www.thesurvivorstrust. org]

The Women's Therapy Centre

> The Women's Therapy Centre has been offering individual and group psychotherapy to women since 1976. Its access policy ensures that psychotherapy is available to all women, regardless of ability to pay, sexual orientation, disability, cultural or social background, immigrant status, previous psychiatric history or age. The

Centre has a particular commitment to offering psychotherapy to women whose needs might not otherwise be met elsewhere. Psychotherapy is also available in languages other than English; interpreters are used within Psychotherapy if necessary.

The Psychotherapy Service

Group and individual psychoanalytic psychotherapy is offered at the Centre, as well as time-limited short term focused groups for women who have experienced sexual abuse in childhood (Grant, Mohamed, & Ruthie Smith, 1993; Sutton Smith, 1992). Psychoanalytic psychotherapy sets out to understand the underlying causes of a wide range of difficulties. These difficulties might sometimes be linked to a particular experience, for example a bereavement or recent or past traumatic event. Other reasons for seeking psychotherapy may be harder to define, for example, problems of depression or low self-esteem. Psychotherapy offers help with following and making sense of thoughts, feelings and ways of relating to oneself and others, within the context of the relationship with the psychotherapist. Psychotherapists do not talk about themselves, or offer practical advice, and the work is confidential.

The Psychotherapists

The Women's Therapy Centre is a member of the United Kingdom Council for Psychotherapy (UKCP). All colleagues receive regular clinical supervision and work to the Code of Ethics of UKCP. The psychotherapists are members of at least one professional registration body, either UKCP or the British Psychoanalytic Council (BPC).

The Centre's psychotherapists have experience of working psychotherapeutically with a full range of issues, including eating-related problems, childhood sexual abuse, self-harm and violent relationships. There is a commitment among the staff of the Centre to ongoing thinking about links between women's internal worlds and their external circumstances. The Centre maintains a culturally diverse staff group.

The Self-Referral Process

Any woman may refer herself by email, phone or in writing, regardless of where she lives. Professionals are welcome to contact the Centre on behalf of a patient or client, but the Centre usually suggests that the woman herself also makes contact, in keeping with the Centre's self-referral policy. Requests for psychotherapy are received by the Centre's Appointments and Referrals office.

Whenever possible, a consultation with a psychotherapist is offered. This may involve a wait of up to four weeks. Waiting lists are kept short in order to minimise delays. When the waiting list for a consultation is closed, the Centre staff will try to suggest an alternative. Although the waiting list often has to be closed, it re-opens frequently as new consultation times become available, so it is worth phoning again to see if the list has re-opened.

The Consultation

Initial consultations are with an experienced psychotherapist and appointments last for fifty minutes. The consultation gives an opportunity to explore the reasons for seeking therapy. Sometimes the psychotherapist will suggest having another meeting if more time is needed to reach a decision. If psychotherapy seems to be the most appropriate form of help, the therapist will arrange a referral for group or individual psychotherapy as discussed. This can be for psychotherapy within the Centre, or outside the Centre with a well-regarded colleague whose work is known to the Centre, depending on what is most appropriate to individual needs. The psychotherapist will discuss the sort of referral she would recommend at the consultation. The exact details of the referral, including a first appointment time, will follow in a letter. There is sometimes a wait for a referral, which the Centre tries to keep to a minimum. The psychotherapist will be able to give an indication of any likely delay while a suitable vacancy is sought.

Starting Psychotherapy

Psychotherapy sessions take place on a weekly basis (sometimes twice weekly), at a regular time. Practical details such as the fee and the length of time for which the therapy space is available, are clarified at the outset. [The Women's Therapy Centre: www.womenstherapycentre.co.uk]

Family Matters

We are Gravesend based charity offering counselling and a helpline to survivors of childhood sexual abuse and rape of any age.

The service is available in SE London (Bexley, Bromley & Greenwich boroughs) and all of Kent down as far as Ashford (Medway, Dartford, Gravesham, Sevenoaks, Tunbridge Wells, Tonbridge and Malling, Swale, Maidstone and Ashford.).

The charity's work is almost solely maintained by charitable grants with only a small proportion of its income coming from statutory sources (Bexley, Greenwich & Medway).

Last year (06/08) we saw 479 clients and took some 3000 calls on our helpline. Demand for our services continues to be high with a current waiting list of 40 clients and a waiting time of 12–16 weeks.

The counselling is time limited to 12 weeks initially, with extensions when a clinical need is identified. The client is put in the driving seat of their therapy and asked from the beginning to set personal goals and self assess their progress. The approach is integrative, using the core condition of empathy, congruence, unconditional positive regard & warmth. Given the time limits, the therapy has to be focused.

Family Matters has around 35–40 volunteer and sessionally paid counsellors who travel to by-the-hour rented High Street locations, a deliberate policy to increase accessibility and make the setting non medical.

The whole operation is overseen by [a] Clinical Manager through a team of 6 specialist supervisors and an on-going self-assessment system which is completed by the client. The entire operation is covered by an extensive Policies and Procedures document and underpinned by the BACP Ethics and Guidelines. All counsellors with Family Matters receive in-house training in sexual abuse awareness and are tutored throughout their time with us by their supervisors.

Birmingham Rape and Sexual Violence Project (formerly Rape Crisis)

Since we acknowledge sexual violence and abuse impacts widely on the survivor *and* the people around them, most of our services are also available to their supporters—partners, families, friends and carers. Also, all our services are available to female *and* male survivors, from the age of 18 years upwards except the advocacy service. The advocacy service is available to children and young people from the age of 14 years upwards, since there is a lack of support for children attending court.

The current services that we provide are:

Telephone helpline. Callers can ring for emotional support, information (for example about where to go to for sexual health testing and on how to cope with flashbacks) & sign posting to other agencies. For some of our long-term callers the support we offer is more like befriending. However, we keep the focus around abuse to avoid clients becoming dependent on us.

Advocacy service delivered by independent advisers. We provide survivors and their families with emotional & practical support to help them deal with the stress and trauma of going through Police & court proceedings. We help people decide whether reporting to the Police is the right thing for them; we go to the Police station with people and support them whilst giving a statement and we also support people when they are giving evidence in court.

One to one counselling. This service is open 7 days a week, so people can access the service at a time to suit them. We have female and male counsellors, so people can choose who they see. We also have counsellors of different ethnicities and are able to offer counselling in some Asian languages. We offer up to 6 months of counselling to survivors and 10 weeks of counselling to their supporters—so they can deal with their own feelings about the abuse and explore ways to support their loved one better.

Visual Evidence for Victims (VEV). Survivors can have photos taken of injuries caused by sexual violence and abuse. These photos can then be used as evidence if the person later reports the crime to the Police. This service is useful for people who might need to build up confidence to speak to the Police. E.g. In cases of domestic violence or for people who work in the sex industry.

Written Self-Help Information Sheets to improve people's coping strategies—for example we provide information about self harm and how to overcome it; how to support someone who has been abused and what happens if you go to court. We also have self-help sheets, including on forced marriage, in 5 South Asian languages for minority victims.

Specialised counselling & support, for female asylum seekers & refugees who have fled their own country due to sexual violence/torture. (Figures show 50–80% of this group are seeking asylum and fleeing their own country due to sexual violence/torture.) We help women deal with the effects of the sexual trauma and support them to settle into this country.

Black and minority ethnic development work. We make links and consult with individuals, agencies and communities, so we can develop more sensitive and culturally appropriate services for Black and minority ethnic survivors.

Education, training & awareness raising. We deliver these sessions to statutory and voluntary agencies. We regularly train the West Midlands Police on the emotional effects of abuse and how to meet the needs of a survivor who has reported to the Police. We have also trained Doctors, Sexual Health workers, Witness Care, Victim Support and Housing workers in the past.

Rugby RoSA (Rape or Sexual Abuse Support Project)

Service Specification

Rugby RoSA exists to provide confidential counselling and support for men, women and young people from the age of 13 years who have experienced Rape or Sexual Abuse, whether it is recent, on-going or historical childhood sexual abuse. We are also able to support family members in the same way. Rugby RoSA also provides a confidential Helpline service on Saturday mornings 10am to 1pm with trained volunteer support workers available. Importantly, callers are offered an assessment within two weeks of contacting RoSA.

The service was initially established over 15 years ago after local community residents identified the dire gap in service provision for all survivors of sexual crimes in this area. Over the years, RoSA has developed its specialist training to equip volunteers and workers with all relevant skills to meet the complex and challenging demands of working with this very vulnerable client group.

RoSA is also has an Independent Sexual Violence Service for clients, which liaises with statutory services on behalf of the client and can accompany when making a statement to the police and advising on court procedures etc.

RoSA operates under the management of a board of trustees and adheres to charity law and financial reporting regulations. With regard to its clinical counselling and support services, RoSA is a member of the British Association for Counselling and Psychotherapy (BACP) and provides its counselling and support services in accordance with their ethical framework. RoSA's counselling and support volunteers also adhere to the RoSA's own Working Policies and Procedures which are specifically tailored to the needs of victims and survivors of sexual violence and childhood sexual abuse.

All RoSA counselling and support volunteers are required to successfully complete 60 hours of specialist in-house training, provide two references and are CRB checked before being accepted into the charity as volunteers. All counselling and support volunteers receive a minimum of 11/2 hours supervision per month, in accordance with BACP guidelines.

RoSA recruits counselling and support volunteers from within the community, providing specialist in-house training and supervision to support their work. Volunteers are drawn from all ages, backgrounds and origins. Volunteers receive no payment for their services and currently do not receive any payment for expenses.

Organizational structure:

RoSA management committee comprises 8 individuals from within the community with a range of skills and experience, including business and financial management, counselling and volunteering.

Staff: Independent Sexual Violence Adviser
            Volunteer Co-ordinator
            Part-time Administrative Worker

Volunteers: 5 Helpline volunteers
              20 Counselling and support volunteers
              2 Supervisors

Service philosophy:

RoSA is a full member of The Survivors' Trust, the national umbrella agency for specialist rape and sexual abuse services, and adheres to the following service philosophy:

Core belief . . .

We believe that the sexual abuse and/or rape of girls, boys, women and men is preventable and we challenge society to acknowledge both its reality and our individual and collective responsibility for it.

RoSA core philosophy and service rationale is based on an ecological framework, which takes account of individual, relationship, community and societal influences, is most helpful in understanding the factors that influence sexual violence and abuse and also provides key points for prevention and intervention.

Core values . . .

RoSA supports working in ways that:

- Recognise human rights and dignity;
- Appreciate the variety of human experience and culture;
- Demonstrate a commitment to showing justice in dealing with all others;
- Encourages continual development and improvement of professional knowledge of its staff, volunteers and trustees.

Direct services to clients:

- Individual counselling and support for victims and survivors
- Individual counselling and support for family members/ partners
- Couple counselling and support
- Group support for women, men and young people
- Helpline
- Independent Sexual Violence Adviser Service
- Risk Assessment
- Child protection advice and support
- Court support
- Advice, information and signposting
- Advocacy
- Mediation
- School Information Sessions as part of PSHE curriculum
- Practical support in accessing other services

Over the past year RoSA has supported 117 individuals, providing over 1,000 hours of specialist counselling and support and 125 hours of specialist clinical supervision.

Our Helpline has dealt with 1,832 calls in that time and our website has been accessed 207 times.

CIS'ters (Childhood Incest Survivors) Service Specification

CIS'ters is a registered charity, run by survivors for survivors, that provides emotional support to females (age 18+) who were sexually abused during childhood by a member of their immediate or extended family.

As of March 2008, the agency is supporting over 750 women from across the UK.

Services include:

- newsletter,
- workshops,
- group meetings,
- information service,
- support service.

The agency recognises the important role that psychotherapy/counselling can have in the healing process and will signpost survivors to other agencies as appropriate.

The agency also campaigns to raise awareness of core issues related to the impact of sexual abuse, and delivers education, training and awareness sessions as part of this aim.

The agency is governed by a Board of Trustees, including those with specialist knowledge, and a Management Team. There are four paid employees and a team of trained volunteers. Service users help drive the agenda forward and are key to the success of the agency.

REFERENCES

Abbass, A. A. (2003). The cost effectiveness of short term dynamic psychotherapy. *Pharamacoeconomics Outcomes Research*, 3(5):535–539.

Abbass, A. A., Hancock, J. T., Henderson, J., & Kisely, S. (2006). Short-term psychodynamic psychotherapies for common mental disorders. *Cochrane Database of Systematic Reviews*, 4. Article No. CD004687.

Ainsworth, M. D., Blehar, M. C., Waters, E., & Wall, S. (1978). *Patterns of Attachment: A Psychological Study of the Strange Situation*. Hillsdale, NJ: Erlbaum.

American Psychiatric Association (2000). *Diagnostic and Statistical Manual of Mental Disorders (4th edn, text revision) (DSM-IV-TR)*. Washington, DC: American Psychiatric Association.

Ammerman, R. T., Lubetsky, M. J., Hersen, M., & Van-Hasselt, V. B. (1988a). Maltreatment of children and adolescents with multiple handicaps: five case examples. *Journal of the Multihandicapped Person*, 1(2):129–139.

Ammerman, R. T., Van Hasselt, V. B., & Hersen, M. (1988b). Maltreatment of handicapped children: a critical review. *Journal of Family Violence*, 3(1): 53–72.

Ammerman, R. T., Van-Hasselt, V. B., Hersen, M., McGonigle, J. J., & Lubetsky, M. J. (1989). Abuse and neglect in psychiatrically

hospitalised multihandicapped children. *Child Abuse and Neglect,*
13(3): 335–343.

Andrews, G., Corry, J., Slade, T., Issakidis, C., & Swanston, H. (2004).
Child sexual abuse. In: M. Ezzati, A. D. Lopez, A. Rodgers, &
C. J. L. Murray (Eds.), *Comparative Quantification of Health Risks:*
Global and Regional Burden of Disease Attributable to Selected Major Risk
Factors Vol. 2 (pp. 1851–1940). Geneva: World Health Organization.

Aquarone, R., & Hughes W. (2005). The history of dissociation and
trauma in the UK and its impact on treatment. In: G. F. Rhoades &
V. Sar (Eds.), *Trauma and Dissociation in a Cross-cultural Perspective:*
Not just a North American Phenomenon (pp. 305–322) New York:
Haworth Press.

Archer, J. (2000). Sex differences in aggression between heterosexual
partners. A meta-analytic review. *Psychological Bulletin, 126:*
651–680.

Arnold, R., Rogers, D., & Cook, D. (1990). Medical problems of adults
who were sexually abused in childhood. *British Medical Journal, 300:*
705–708.

Baker, A. W., & Duncan S. P. (1985). Child sexual abuse: a study of
prevalence in Great Britain. *Child Abuse and Neglect, 9:* 457–467.

Bateman, A., & Fonagy, P. (1999). Effectiveness of partial hospitalization in the treatment of borderline personality disorder—a randomized controlled trial. *American Journal of Psychiatry, 156*(10): 1563–
1569.

Bateman, A., & Fonagy, P. (2003). Health service utilization costs for
borderline personality disorder patients treated with psychoanalytically orientated partial hospitalisation versus general psychiatric
care. *American Journal of Psychiatry, 160*(1): 1169–1171.

Beecham, J., Sleed, M., Knapp, M., Chiesa, M., & Drahorad, C. (2006).
The costs and effectiveness of two psychosocial treatment programmes for personality disorder: a controlled study. *European Psychiatry, 21:* 102–109.

Bentovim, A., & Williams, B. (1998). Children and adolescents: victims
who become perpetrators. *Advances in Psychiatric Treatment, 4:*
101–107.

Bifulco, A., Brown, G. W., & Adler, Z. (1991). Early sexual abuse and
clinical depression in adult life. *British Journal of Psychiatry, 159:*
115–122.

Black, N. (1996). Why we need observational studies to evaluate the
effectiveness of health care. *British Medical Journal, 312:* 1215–1218.

Bliss, E. S., & Jeppsen, A. (1985). Prevalence of multiple personality among inpatients and outpatients. *American Journal of Psychiatry*, 142(2): 250–251.

Blunden, S. L., & Carter, J. (2007). *Integrated Systemic Therapy for Traumatised Children and Young People*. London: Childhood First. www.childhoodfirst.org.uk

Bollas, C. (1987). *The Shadow of the Object: Psychoanalysis of the Unthought Known*. London: Free Association.

Bower, P., & Gilbody, S. (2005). Stepped care in psychological therapies: access effectiveness and efficiency. Narrative literature review. *British Journal of Psychiatry*, 186: 11–17.

Bowlby, J. (1969). *Attachment and Loss* (vol. 1): *Attachment*. London: Hogarth.

Bowlby, J. (1973). *Attachment and Loss* (vol. 2): *Separation: Anxiety and Anger*. London: Hogarth.

Bowlby, J. (1980). *Attachment and Loss* (vol. 3): *Loss: Sadness and Depression*. London: Hogarth.

Bradford, J. M. W., Bloomberg, D., & Bourget, D. (1988). The heterogeneity/homogeneity of pedophilia. *Psychiatric Journal of the University of Ottawa*, 13: 217–226.

Brewin, C. R., & Bradley, C. (1989). Patient preferences and randomised clinical trials. *British Medical Journal*, 299: 313–315.

Brown, G. W., Craig, T. K. J., Harris, T. O., & Handley, R. V. (2008). Parental maltreatment and adult cohabiting partnerships: A life course study of chronic depression—4. *Journal of Affective Disorders*, (in press).

Brown, G. W., Craig, T. K. J., Harris, T. O. Handley, R.V., & Harvey, A. L. (2007a). Development of a retrospective interview measure of parental maltreatment using the Childhood Experience of Care and Abuse (CECA) instrument—a life-course study of adult chronic depression—1. *Journal of Affective Disorders*, 103, 205–215.

Brown, G. W., Craig, T. K. J., Harris, T. O., Handley, R. V., & Harvey, A. L. (2007b). Validity of retrospective measures of early maltreatment and depressive episodes using the Childhood Experience of Care and Abuse (CECA) instrument: a life-course study of adult chronic depression—2. *Journal of Affective Disorders*, 103: 217–224.

Brown, G. W., Craig, T. K. J., Harris, T. O., Handley, R. V., & Harvey, A. L. (2007c). Child-specific and family-wide risk factors using the Childhood Experience of Care and Abuse (CECA) instrument: a life-course study of chronic depression—3. *Journal of Affective Disorders*, 103: 225–236.

Brunner, R., Parzer, P., Schuld, V., & Resch, F. (2000). Dissociative symptomatology and traumatogenic factors in adolescent psychiatric patients. *Journal of Nervous and Mental Disease, 188*: 71–77.

Buchanan, A., & Oliver, J. E. (1979). Abuse and neglect as a cause of mental retardation. *Child Abuse and Neglect, 3*: 467–475.

Buchanan, A., & Wilkins, R. (1991). Sexual abuse of the mentally handicapped. *Psychiatric Bulletin, 15*: 601–605.

Bulik, C. M., Prescott, C. A., Kendler, K. S. (2001). Features of childhood sexual abuse and the development of psychiatric and substance use disorders. *British Journal of Psychiatry, 179*: 444–449.

Bunting, L. (2005). *Females Who Sexually Offend Against Children: Responses of the Child Protection and Criminal Justice Systems.* London: NSPCC.

Bunting, L. (2007). Dealing with a problem that doesn't exist? Professional responses to female perpetrated child sexual abuse. *Child Abuse Review, 16*: 252–267.

Cabinet Office Social Exclusion Task Force (2006a). *Reaching Out: An Action Plan on Social Exclusion.* London: Cabinet Office.

Cabinet Office Social Exclusion Task Force (2006b). *Reaching Out: Think Family. Analysis and Themes from the Families at Risk Review.* London: Cabinet Office.

Cabinet Office Social Exclusion Task Force (2008). *Think Family: Improving the Life Chances of Families at Risk.* London: Cabinet Office.

Caplan, P. J., & Dinardo, L. (1986). Is there a relationship between child abuse and learning disability? Special Issue: Family violence, child abuse, and wife assault. *Canadian Journal of Behavioural Science, 1894)*: 367–380.

Cawson, P., Wattam, C., Brooker, S., & Kelly, G. (2000). *Child Maltreatment in the UK: A Study of Prevalence of Child Abuse and Neglect.* London: NSPCC.

Centre for Economic Performance's Mental Health Policy Group (2006). *The Depression Report: A New Deal for Depression and Anxiety Disorders.* London School of Economics, Centre for Economic Performance. http:cep.lse.ac.uk/textonly/research/mentalhealth/DEPRESSION_REPORT_LAYARD.pdf

CEOP (2007). *A Scoping Project on Child Trafficking in the UK. Making every child matter . . . everywhere.* London: Child Exploitation and Online Protection Centre. CEOP: www.ceop.gov.uk

Chiesa, M., Fonagy, P., Holmes, J., & Drahorad, C. (2004). Residential versus community treatment of personality disorders: A comparative study of three treatment programmes. *American Journal of Psychiatry, 161*(8): 1463–1470.

Chiesa, M., Fonagy, P., Holmes, J., Drahorad, C., & Harrison-Hall, A. (2002). Health service use costs by personality disorder following specialist and non-specialist treatment: a comparative study. *Journal of Personality Disorders, 16*(2): 160–173.

Chu, J. A. (1998). *Rebuilding Shattered Lives. The Responsible Treatment of Complex Post-traumatic and Dissociative Disorders*. New York: Wiley.

Clarkin, J. F., Levy, K. N., Lenzenweger, M. F., & Kernberg, O. F. (2007). Evaluating three treatments for borderline personality disorder: A multiwave study. *The American Journal of Psychiatry, 164*(6): 922–928.

Coons, P. M. (1996). Clinical phenomenology of 25 children and adolescents with dissociative disorders. *Child and Adolescent Psychiatric Clinics of North America, 5*: 361–374.

Coxell, A., King, M., Mezey, G., & Gordon, D. (1999). Lifetime prevalence, characteristics, and associated problems of non-consensual sex in men: cross sectional survey. *British Medical Journal, 318*: 846–850.

Cozolino, L. (2002). *The Neuroscience of Psychotherapy. Building and Rebuilding the Human Brain*. New York: W. W. Norton.

Craft, A., & Craft, M. (1981). Sexuality and mental handicap: a review. *British Journal of Psychiatry, 139*: 494–505.

Davies, M., Pollard, P., & Archer, J. (2006). Effects of perpetrator gender and victim sexuality on blame toward male victims of sexual assault. *Journal of Social Psychology, 146*(3): 275–291.

Dell, P. F., & Eisenhower, J. W. (1990). Adolescent multiple personality disorder: A preliminary study of eleven cases. *Journal of the American Academy of Child and Adolescent Psychiatry, 29*: 359–366.

Department for Children, Schools and Families (2007). *Referrals, Assessments and Children and Young People Who Are the Subject of a Child Protection Plan or Are on Child Protection Registers, England—Year Ending 31 March 2007*. London: The Stationery Office.

Department for Education and Skills (2006). *Working Together to Safeguard Children. A Guide to Inter-agency Working to Safeguard and Promote the Welfare of Children*. London: Department for Education and Skills.

Department for Education and Skills (2007). *Safeguarding Children from Abuse Linked to a Belief in Spirit Possession*. London: Department for Education and Skills.

Department of Health (2000). *The Same as You? A Review of Services for People with Learning Disabilities*. London: Department of Health.

Department of Health (2001a). *Valuing People: A New Strategy for Learn-ing Disability for the 21st Century.* London: Department of Health.

Department of Health (2001b). *Guidelines on Treatment Choice in Psycho-logical Therapies and Counselling.* London: Department of Health.

Department of Health (2003). *Mainstreaming Gender and Women's Mental Health: Implementation Guidance.* London: Department of Health.

Department of Health (2004). *Organising and Delivering Psychological Therapies.* London: Department of Health.

Department of Health (2007). *Improving Access to Psychological Therapies: Positive Practice Guide: Commissioning a Brighter Future.* London: Department of Health.

Department of Health, Children and Mental Health Division and Home Office (2005). *Developing Sexual Assault Referral Centres (SARCs)— National Service Guidelines.* London: Department of Health.

de Zulueta, F. (1999). Borderline personality disorder as seen from an attachment perspective: a review. *Criminal Behaviour and Mental Health, 9*: 237–253.

de Zulueta, F. (2002). From post traumatic stress disorder to dissociative identity disorder: the traumatic stress service in the Maudsley Hos-pital. In: V. Sinason (Ed.), *Attachment Trauma and Multiplicity, Work - ing with Dissociative Identity Disorder* London: Brunner-Routledge.

de Zulueta, F. (2006). The treatment of psychological trauma from the perspective of attachment research. *Journal of Family Therapy, 28*: 334–351.

Diamond, L. J., & Jaudes, P. K. (1983). Child abuse in a cerebral palsied population. *Developmental Medicine and Child Neurology, 26*: 169–174.

Dozier, M., Stovall, K. C., & Albus, K. E. (1999). Attachment and psychopathology in adulthood. In: J. Cassidy & P. R. Shaver (Eds.), *Handbook of Attachment: Theory, Research, and Clinical Applications* (pp. 497–519). New York: Guilford.

Duggal, S., & Sroufe, L. A. (1989). Recovered memory of childhood sexual trauma: a documented case from a longitudinal study. *Journal of Traumatic Stress, 11*: 301–321.

Durham, R. C., Chambers, J. A., Power, K. G., Sharp, D. M., Macdonald, R. R., Major, K. A., Dow, M. T. G., & Gumley, A. I. (2005). Long-term outcome of cognitive behaviour therapy clinical trials in central Scotland. *Health Technology Assessment, 9*: 42.

Edwards, H. (2005). *Faith, Religion and Safeguarding.* NSPCC Internal Briefing Paper, revised 2007. NSPCC. (http://www.nspcc.org.uk/ Inform/trainingandconsultancy/Consultancy/HelpAndAdvice/ FaithReligionAndSafeguarding_wdf47840.pdf)

Elwood, S. (1981). Sex and the mentally handicapped. *Bulletin of the British Psychological Society, 34*: 169–171.

Egeland, B., Jacobvitz, D., & Papatola, K. (1987) Intergenerational continuity of parental abuse. In: R. J. Gelles & J. B. Lancaster (Eds.), *Child Abuse and Neglect*. New York: Aldine de Gruyter.

Egeland, B., Jacobvitz, D., & Sroufe, L. A. (1988). Breaking the cycle of abuse. *Child Development, 59*: 1080–1088.

Fairbairn, W. R. D. (1952). *Psychoanalytic Studies of the Personality*. London: Routledge.

Felitti, V. J., Anda, R. F., Nordenberg, D., Williamson, D. F., Spitz, A. M., Edwards, V., Koss, M. P., & Marks, J. S. (1998). Relationship of childhood abuse and household dysfunction to many of the leading causes of death in adults: the Adverse Childhood Experiences (ACE) Study. *American Journal of Preventative Medicine, 14*(4): 245–258.

Finkelhor, D. (1994a). The international epidemiology of child sexual abuse. *Child Abuse and Neglect, 18*: 409–417.

Finkelhor, D. (1994b). Current information on the scope and nature of child sexual abuse. The future of children. *Sexual Abuse of Children, 4*: 2:31–53.

Finkelhor, D., & Berliner, L. (1995). Research on the treatment of sexually abused children: A review and recommendations. *Journal of the American Academy of Child and Adolescent Psychiatry, 34*(11): 1408–1423.

Fleming, J. M. (1997). Prevalence of childhood sexual abuse in a community sample of Australian women. *Medical Journal of Australia, 166*: 65–68.

Flood-Page, C., & Taylor, J. (Eds.) (2003). *Crime in England and Wales 2001/2002: Supplementary Volume*. London: Home Office.

Fonagy, P. (Ed.) (2002). *An Open Door Review of Outcome Studies in Psychoanalysis* (2nd edn, revised). London: International Psychoanalytic Association.

Fonagy, P., & Bateman A. (2006). Editorial: progress in the treatment of borderline personality disorder. *British Journal of Psychiatry, 188*: 1–3.

Fonagy, P., & Target, M. (1995). Dissociation and trauma. *Current Opinion in Psychiatry, 8*: 161–166.

Fonagy, P., & Target, M. (1997). Attachment and reflective function: their role in self organisation. *Development and Psychopathology, 9*: 679–700.

Fonagy, P., Gergely, G., Jurist, E., & Target, M. (2004). *Affect Regulation, Mentalization, and the Development of the Self*. London: Karnac.

104 REFERENCES

Fonagy, P., Leigh, T., Steele, M., Steele, H., Kennedy, R., Mattoon, G., Target, M., & Gerber, A. (1996). The relation of attachment status, psychiatric classification, and response to psychotherapy. *Journal of Consulting and Clinical Psychology, 64*(1): 22–31.

Fonagy, P., Steele, H., & Steele, M. (1991). Maternal representations of attachment during pregnancy predict the organization of infant–mother attachment at one year of age. *Child Development, 62*: 891–905.

Foote, B., Smolin, Y., Neft, D. I., & Lipschitz, D. (2008). Dissociative disorders and suicidality in psychiatric outpatients. *Journal of Nervous & Mental Disease, 196*(1): 29–36.

Friedl, M. C., & Draijer, N. (2000). Dissociative disorders in Dutch psychiatric inpatients. *American Journal of Psychiatry, 157*: 1012–1013.

Friedl, M. C., Draijer, N., & de Jonge, P. (2000). Prevalence of dissociative disorders in psychiatric in-patients: the impact of study characteristics. *Acta Psychiatrica Scandinavica, 102*(6): 423–428.

Gabbard, G. O. (2005). *Psychodynamic Psychiatry in Clinical Practice*. Washington, DC: American Psychiatric Publishing.

Garbarino, J. (1987). The abuse and neglect of special children. In: J. Garbarino, P. E. Brookhouser, & K. J. Authier (Eds.), *Special Children Special Risks* (pp. 3–16). New York: Aldine de Gruyter.

Gaskell, C. (2008) *"Kids Company Helps with the Whole Problem": A Research and Evaluation Analysis of Kids Company*. London: Kids Company and Queen Mary College, University of London.

Goff, D. C., Olin, J. A., Jenike, M. A., Baer, L., & Buttolph, M. L. (1992). Dissociative symptoms in patients with obsessive-compulsive disorder. *Journal of Nervous and Mental Disease, 180*: 332–337.

Grant, R., Mohamed, C., & Ruthie Smith, R. (1993). *Time-Limited Psychotherapy at the Women's Therapy Centre: A Guide to Practice*. London: Women's Therapy Centre.

Greenberg, M. T. (1999). Attachment and psychopathology in childhood. In: J. Cassidy & P. R. Shaver (Eds.), *Handbook of Attachment: Theory, Research, and Clinical Applications* (pp 469–496). New York: Guilford.

Grubin, D. (1998). *Sex Offending Against Children: Understanding the Risk*. Police Research Series Paper 99. London: Home Office.

Hanmer, J., & Itzin, C. (2000). *Home Truths About Domestic Violence*. London: Routledge.

Hard, S., & Plumb, W. (1987). Sexual abuse of persons with developmental disabilities: a case study. Unpublished manuscript annotated in Brown, H., & Turk, V. (1991) *Sexual Abuse and People with*

Learning Difficulties: Annotated Bibliography. Canterbury: University of Kent at Canterbury Centre for Applied Psychology of Social Care.

Haseltine, B., & Miltenberger, R. (1990). Teaching self-protection skills to persons with mental retardation. *American Journal on Mental Retardation, 95*(2): 188–197.

Hawton, K., Rodham, K., Evans, E., & Weatherall, R. (2002). Deliberate self-harm in adolescents: self report survey in schools in England. *British Medical Journal, 325*(7374):1207–1211.

Healy, K., & Kennedy, R. (1993). Which families benefit from inpatient psychotherapeutic work at the Cassel Hospital? *British Journal of Psychotherapy, 9:* 394–404.

Healy, K., Kennedy, R., & Sinclair, J. (1991). Child physical abuse observed: comparison of families with and without history of child abuse treated in an in-patient family unit. *British Journal of Psychiatry, 158:* 234–237.

Henderson, L. (2003). *Prevalence of Domestic Violence among Lesbians and Gay Men.* Portsmouth: Data Report to Flame TV.

Herman, J. L. (1992). Complex PTSD. A syndrome in survivors of prolonged and repeated trauma. *Journal of Traumatic Stress, 5:* 377–391.

Hester, M., Pearson, C., & Harwin, N. (2000). *Making an Impact: Children and Domestic Violence—A Reader.* London: Jessica Kingsley.

Hetherton, J., & Beardsall, L. (1998). Decisions and attitudes concerning child sexual abuse: does the gender of the perpetrator make a difference to child protection professionals? *Child Abuse and Neglect, 22*(12): 1265–1283.

Hewitt, S. K. (1987). The abuse of deinstitutionalised persons with mental handicaps. *Disability, Handicap and Society, 2*(2): 127–135.

Hickey, N., Vizard, E., McCrory, E., & French, L. (2006). Links between juvenile sexually abusive behaviour and emerging severe personality disorder traits in childhood. London: Department of Health.

Hindman, J., & Peters, J. M. (2001). Polygraph testing leads to better understanding adult and juvenile sex offenders. *Federal Probation, 65*(3): 8–15.

HM Government (2004). *Every Child Matters: Change for Children.* London: Department for Education and Skills.

Hofer, M. A. (1995). Hidden regulators: implications for a new understanding of attachment, separation and loss. In: S. Goldberg, R. Muir, & J. Kerr (Eds.), *Attachment Theory: Social, Developmental and Clinical Perspectives* (pp. 203–230). Hillsdale, NJ: Analytic Press.

Hornstein, N. L., & Putnam, F. W. (1992). Clinical phenomenology of child and adolescent dissociative disorders. *Journal of the American Academy of Child and Adolescent Psychiatry, 31*: 1077–1085.

Hopper, E. (2002). Commentary on Sinason, V. (2002). *Treating People with Learning Disability after Physical or Sexual Abuse. Advances in Psychiatric Treatment, 8*: 424–432.

Humphreys, C., & Thiara, R. (2003). Mental health and domestic violence: 'I call it symptoms of abuse'. *British Journal of Social Work, 33*: 209–226.

IS (2006). Believe. *Rainbows End—Support and Information Newsletter of First Person Plural,* 6: 4: 5.

Itzin, C. (2000). *Home Truths About Domestic Violence.* London: Routledge.

Itzin, C. (2006). *Tackling the Health and Mental Health Effects of Domestic and Sexual Violence and Abuse.* London: Joint Department of Health and National Institute for Mental Health in England (NIMHE).

Itzin, C. (work in progress). *Tackling the Root Causes of Mental Illness in Domestic and Sexual Violence and Abuse: A Compendium of Guidelines and Information on Therapeutic and Preventive Interventions with Victims, Survivors & Abusers, Children, Adolescents & Adults.*

James, B., & Nasjleti, M. (1983). *Treating Sexually Abused Children and their Families.* Palo Alto, CA: Consulting Psychologists Press.

Johnson, J. G., Cohen, P., Smailes, E. M., Skodol, A. E., Brown, J., & Oldham, J. M. (2001). Childhood verbal abuse and risk for personality disorders during adolescence and early adulthood. *Comprehensive Psychiatry, 42*(1): 16–23.

Jones, P. H., & Ramchandani, P. (1999). *Child Sexual Abuse, Informing Practice from Research.* Abingdon: Radcliffe Medical Press.

Kelly, L., Regan, L., & Burton, S. (1991). *An Exploratory Study of the Prevalence of Sexual Abuse in a Sample of 16- to 21-year-olds.* London: Child Abuse Studies Unit, Polytechnic of North London. (Available from cwasu.org)

Kendall-Tackett, K. A., Williams, L. M., & Finkelhor, D. (1993). Impact of sexual abuse of children: a review and synthesis of recent empirical studies. *Psychological Bulletin, 113*: 164–180.

Kennedy, M. (1990). No more secrets. *Deafness Journal, 6*(1): 10–12.

Kennedy, R. (1996). Bearing the unbearable—working with the abused mind. *Psychoanalytic Psychotherapy, 10*(2): 143–154 [reprinted in *The Many Voices of Psychoanalysis.* London: Routledge, 2007].

Kennedy, R. (1997). *Child Abuse, Psychotherapy and the Law.* London: Free Association.

Kennedy, R., Heymans, A., & Tischler L. (Eds.) (1987). *The Family As In-patient. Working with Families and Adolescents at the Cassel Hospital.* London: Free Association.

Kessler, R. C., Molnar, B. E., Feurer, I. D., & Appelbaum, M. (2001). Patterns and mental health predictors of domestic violence in the United States. Results from the National Comorbidity Survey. *International Journal of Law and Psychiatry, 24:* 487–508.

Kitzmann, K. M., Gaylord, N. K., Holt, A. R., & Kenny, E. D. (2003). Child witnesses to domestic violence: a meta-analytic review. *Journal of Consulting and Clinical Psychology, 71:* 339–352.

Kvam, M. H. (2004). Sexual abuse of deaf children. A retrospective analysis of the prevalence and characteristics of childhood sexual abuse among deaf adults in Norway. *Child Abuse and Neglect, 28(3):* 241–251.

Lab, D., Santos, I., & de Zulueta, F. (2008). Treating post traumatic stress disorder in the "real world:": evaluation of a specialist trauma service and adaptations to standard treatment approaches. *Psychiatric Bulletin, 32:* 8–12.

Langhinrichsen-Rohling, D., & Vivian, J. (1994). Are bi-directionally violent couples mutually victimized? A gender-sensitive comparison. *Violence and Victims, 9:*107–124.

Latz, T. T., Kramer, S. I., & Highes, D. L. (1995). Multiple personality disorder among female inpatients in a state hospital. *American Journal of Psychiatry, 152:* 1343–1348.

Leserman, J. (2005). Sexual abuse history: prevalence, health effects, mediators and psychological treatment. *Psychosomatic Medicine, 67:* 906–915.

Liotti, G. (1995). Disorganized/disoriented attachment in the psychotherapy of the dissociative disorders. In: S. Goldberg, R. Muir, & J. Kerr (Eds.), *Attachment Theory: Social, Developmental and Clinical Perspectives* (pp. 343–363). Hillsdale, NJ: Analytic Press.

Lovell, E. (2002a). *"I Think I Might Need some more Help with this Problem . . ." Responding to Children and Young People Who Display Sexually Harmful Behaviour.* London: NSPCC Publications.

Lovell, E. (2002b). *Children and Young People Who Display Sexually Harmful Behaviour.* http://www.nspcc.org.uk/Inform/research/Briefings

MacDonald, J., Sinason, V., & Hollins, S. (2003). An interview study of people with learning disabilities' experience of, and satisfaction with, group analytic therapy. *Psychology and Psychotherapy. Theory, Research and Practice, 76:* 433–453.

Mace, C. (Ed.) (1995). *The Art and Science of Assessment in Psychotherapy.* London: Routledge.

MacFie, J., Cicchetti, D., & Toth, S. L. (2001). The development of dissociation in maltreated preschool children. *Development and Psychopathology, 13:* 223–254.

MacMillan, H. L., Fleming, J. E., Streiner, D. L., Lin, E., Boyle, M. H., Jamieson, E., Duku, E. K., Walsh, C. A., Wong, M. Y. Y., & Beardslee, W. R. (2001). Childhood abuse and lifetime psychopathology in a community sample. *American Journal of Psychiatry, 158:* 1878–1883.

Main, M., & Hess, E. (1992). Disorganised/disorientated infant behaviour in the Strange Situation, lapses in monitoring of reasoning and discourse during the parent's Adult Attachment Interview, and dissociative states. In: M. Ammanati & D. Stern (Eds.), *Attachment and Psychoanalysis* (pp. 86–140). Rome: Gius Laterza and Figli.

Main, M., & Solomon, J. (1990). Procedures for identifying infants as disorganized/disoriented during the Ainsworth Strange Situation. In: M. T. Greenberg, D. Cicchetti, & E. M. Cummings (Eds.), *Attachment in the Preschool Years* (pp. 121–160). Chicago, IL: University of Chicago Press.

Main, T. (1981). The concept of the therapeutic community. In: Main, T. (1998). *The Ailment and Other Psychoanalytic Essays.* London: Free Association.

Malan, D. H. (2004). *Individual Psychotherapy and the Science of Psychodynamics* (2nd edn). London: Arnold.

Mama, A. (2000). Violence against black women in the home. In: J. Hanmer, & C. Itzin (Eds.) *Home Truths About Domestic Violence* (pp. 44–57). London: Routledge.

McCallum, K. E., Lock, J., Kulla, M., Rorty, M., & Wetzel, R. D. (1992). Dissociative symptoms and disorders in patients with eating disorders. *Dissociation, 5:* 227–235.

McCarthy, M., & Thompson, D. (1992). *Sex and the Three Rs, Rights, Responsibilities and Risks: A Sex Education Package for Working with People with Learning Difficulties.* Brighton: Pavilion.

Mind (2002). *My Choice.* www.mind.org.uk

Mirrlees-Black, C. (1999). *Findings from a New British Crime Survey Self-completion Questionnaire.* Home Office Research Study 191. London: Home Office.

Modestin, J., Ebner, G., Junghan, M., & Erni, T. (1995). Dissociative experiences and dissociative disorders in acute psychiatric inpatients. *Comprehensive Psychiatry, 37*(5): 355–361.

Morgan, C., & Fisher, H. (2007). Environment and schizophrenia: environmental factors in schizophrenia: childhood trauma—a critical review. *Schizophrenia Bulletin*, *33*(1): 3–10.

Morrison, Z. (2007). *Feeling Heavy: Vicarious Trauma and Other Issues Facing Those Who Work in the Sexual Assault Field*. Australian Centre for the Study of Sexual Assault, Wrap 4. Australian Institute of Family Studies.

Mrazek, P. J., Lynch, M. A., & Bentovim, A. (1983). Sexual abuse of children in the United Kingdom. *Child Abuse and Neglect*, 7: 147–153.

Mullen, P. E., Martin, J. L., Anderson, J. C., Romans, S. E., & Herbison, G. P. (1996). The long-term impact of the physical, emotional, and sexual abuse of children: a community study. *Child Abuse and Neglect*, *20*: 7–21.

Mullen, P. E., Roman-Clarkson, S. E., & Walton, V. A. (1988). Impact of sexual and physical abuse on women's mental health. *Lancet*, *1*: 841–845.

Mullender, A. (2004). *Tackling Domestic Violence: Providing Support for Children Who Have Witnessed Domestic Violence*. Development and Practice Report 33. London: Home Office.

Mullender, A., & Morley, R. (1994). *Children Living with Domestic Violence*. London: Whiting and Birch.

Murphy, P. E. (1994). Dissociative experiences and dissociative disorders in a non-clinical university student group. *Dissociation*, *7*(1): 28–34.

National Institute for Mental Health in England (NIMHE) (2003). *Personality Disorder: No Longer a Diagnosis of Exclusion. Policy Implementation Guideline for the Development of Services for People with a Diagnosis of Personality Disorder*. London: Department of Health.

National Institute for Mental Health in England (NIMHE) *Mental Health Trusts Collaboration Project:* http://www.nimhe.csip.org.uk/our-work/gender-and-womens-mental-health/mental-health-trusts-collaboration-project.html

NCH (2004). *Exploring the Work of NCH Specialist Child Sexual Abuse Projects*. London: NCH.

Nemeroff, C. B., Heim, C. M., Thase, M. E., Klein, D. N., Rush, J., Schatzberg, A. F., Ninan, P. T., McCullough, J. P., Weiss, P. M., Dunner, D. L., Rothbaum, B. O., Kornstein, S., Keitner, G., & Keller, M. B. (2003). Differential responses to psychotherapy versus pharmacotherapy in patients with chronic forms of major depression and childhood trauma. *Proceedings of the National Academy of Science*, *100*(2)4 :14293–14296.

Ney, P. G., Fung, T., & Wickett, A. R. (1994). The worst combinations of child abuse and neglect. *Child Abuse and Neglect, 18*(9): 705–714.

Ney, P. N., & Peters, A. (1995). *Ending the Cycle of Abuse, the Stories of Women Abused as Children and the Group Therapy Techniques that Helped them Heal.* New York: Brunner/Mazel.

NICE (2004) *Guidelines on Self Harm.* London: National Institute of Clinical Excellence.

Nicholas, S., Povey, D., Walker, A., & Kershaw, C. (2005). *Crime in England and Wales 2004/2005.* London: Home Office Statistical Bulletin.

Noll, J. G., Horowitz, L. A., Bonanno, G. A., Trickett, P. K., & Putnam, F. W. (2003a). Revictimization and self-harm in females who experienced childhood sexual abuse: results from a prospective study. *Journal of Interpersonal Violence, 18*(12): 1452–1471.

Noll, J. G., Trickett, P. K., & Putnam, F. W. (2003b). A prospective investigation of the impact of childhood sexual abuse on the development of sexuality. *Journal of Consulting and Clinical Psychology, 71*(3): 575–586.

Noll, J. G., Zeller, M. H., Trickett, P. K., & Putnam, F. W. (2007). Obesity risk for female victims of childhood sexual abuse: a prospective study. *Pediatrics, 120*(1): 61–67.

O'Day, B. (1983). *Preventing Sexual Abuse of Persons with Disabilities: A Curriculum for Hearing Impaired, Physically Disabled, Blind and Mentally Retarded Students.* Santa Cruz, CA: Network Publications.

O'Leary, K. D., Barling, J., Arias, I., Rosenbaum, A., Malone, J., & Tyree, A. (1989). Prevalence and stability of physical aggression between spouses. A longitudinal analysis. *Journal of Consulting and Clinical Psychology, 57*: 263–268.

Ogawa, J. R., Sroufe, L. A., Weinfield, N. S., Carlson, E. A., & Egeland, B. (1997). Development and the fragmented self: longitudinal study of dissociative symptomatology in a nonclinical sample. *Development and Psychopathology, 9*: 855–979.

Oliver, B. E. (2007). Preventing female-perpetrated sexual abuse. *Trauma, Violence and Abuse, 8*(1): 19–32.

Oliver, J. (1988). Successive generations of child maltreatment. *British Journal of Psychiatry, 153*: 543–553.

Oliver, J. (1993). Intergenerational transmission of child abuse: rates, research and clinical implications. *The American Journal of Psychiatry, 150*(9): 1315–1324.

Panksepp, J., & Bernatzky, G. (2002). Emotional sounds and the brain: the neuro-affective foundations of musical appreciation. *Behavioural Processes, 60*: 133–155.

Paolucci, E. O., Genuis, M. L., & Violato, C. (2001). A meta-analysis of the published research on the effects of child sexual abuse. *Journal of Psychology, 135*: 17–36.

Patel, P. (2000). Southall Black Sisters: domestic violence campaigns and alliances across the divisions of race, gender and class. In: J. Hanmer & C. Itzin, C. (Eds.), *Home Truths About Domestic Violence* (pp. 167–185). London: Routledge.

PDM Task Force (2006). *Psychodynamic Diagnostic Manual.* Silver Spring, MD: Alliance of Psychoanalytic Organizations.

Perry, B. D., Pollard, R. A., Bajer, W. L., Sturges, C., Vigilandte, D., & Blakley, T. L. (1995). Continuous heart rate monitoring in maltreated children. *Proceedings of the Annual Meeting of the American Academy of Child and Adolescent Psychiatry, New Research, 21*: 69.

Ramchandani, P., & Jones, P. H. (2003). Treating psychological symptoms in sexually abused children from research findings to service provision. *British Journal of Psychiatry, 183*: 484–490.

Rauch, S. L., van der Kolk, B. A., Fisler, R. E., Alpert, N. M., Orr, S. P., Savage, C. R., Fischman, A. J., Jenike, M. A., & Pitman, R. K. (1996). A symptom provocation study of post traumatic stress disorder using positron emission tomography and script driven imagery. *Archives of General Psychiatry, 53*: 380–387.

Read, J. (1998). Child abuse and severity of disturbance among adult psychiatric inpatients. *Child Abuse and Neglect, 22*(5): 359–363.

Reiser, R., & Mason, M. (1990). *Disability Equality in the Classroom: A Human Rights Issue.* London: Inner London Education Authority.

Ricks, D. (1990). Mental handicap. In: H. Wolff, A. Bateman, & D. Sturgeon (Eds.), *UCH Textbook of Psychiatry* (pp. 517–535). London: Duckworth.

Rind, B., Tromovitch, P., & Bauserman, R. (1998). A meta-analytic examination of assumed properties of child sexual abuse using college samples. *Psychological Bulletin, 124*(1): 22–53.

Rogers, P., & Davies, M. (2007). Perceptions of victims and perpetrators in a depicted child sexual abuse case: gender and age factors. *Journal of Interpersonal Violence, 22*(5): 566–584.

Romans, S., Belaise, C., Martin, J., Morris, E., & Raffi, A. (2002). Childhood abuse and later medical disorders in women. An epidemiological study. *Psychotherapy and Psychosomatics, 71*(3): 141–150.

Ross, C. A. (1991). Epidemiology of multiple personality disorder and dissociation. Psychiatric *Clinics of North America, 14*: 503–517.

Ross, C. A., Anderson, G., Fleisher, W. P., & Norton, G. R. (1991). The frequency of multiple personality disorder among psychiatric inpatients. *American Journal of Psychiatry, 150*: 1717–1720.

Ross, C. A., Kronson, J., Doensgen, S., Barkman, K., Clark, P., & Rockman, G. (1992). Dissociative comorbidity in 100 chemically dependent patients. *Hospital and Community Psychiatry, 43*: 840–842.

Roth, A., & Fonagy, P. (2005). *What Works for Whom? A Critical Review of Psychotherapy Research* (2nd edn). New York: Guilford.

Royal College of Psychiatrists (1997). *Meeting the Mental Health Needs of People with Learning Disability* (Council Report CR56). London: Royal College of Psychiatrists.

Royal College of Psychiatrists (2004). *Psychotherapy and Learning Disability*. Council Report CR116. London: Royal College of Psychiatrists.

Royal College of Psychiatrists & British Psychological Society (1995). *Psychological Therapies for Adults in the NHS* (Council Report CR37). London: Royal College of Psychiatrists.

Royal College of Psychiatrists & British Psychological Society (2005). *Post-traumatic Stress Disorder. The Management of PTSD in Adults and Children in Primary and Secondary Care. National Clinical Practice Guideline Number 26. National Collaborating Centre for Mental Health.* London: Gaskell and the British Psychological Society.

Rutter, M., Tizard, J., & Whitmore, K. (1970). *Education, Health and Behaviour*. London: Longmans.

Ryle, A. (1997). The structure and development of borderline personality disorder: a proposed model. *British Journal of Psychiatry, 170*: 82–87.

Sanders, B., & Giolas, M. H. (1991). Dissociation and childhood trauma in psychologically disturbed adolescents. *American Journal of Psychiatry, 148*: 50–54.

Saxe, G. N., van der Kolk, B. A., Berkowitz, R., Chinman, G., Hall, K., Leiberg, G., & Schwartz, J. (1993). Dissociative disorders in psychiatric inpatients. *American Journal of Psychiatry, 152*: 1037–1042.

Scharff, J. S., & Scharff, D. E. (1994). *Object Relations Therapy of Physical and Sexual Trauma*. Hillsdale, NJ: Lawrence Erlbaum.

Schore, A. N. (1994). *Affect Regulation and the Origin of the Self: The Neurobiology of Emotional Development*. Hillsdale, NJ: Lawrence Erlbaum.

Schore, A. N. (1996). Experience dependent maturation of a regulatory system in the orbito-frontal cortex and the origin of developmental psychopathology. *Development and Psychopathology, 8*: 59–87.

Schore, A. N. (2002). Dysregulation of the right brain: a fundamental mechanism of traumatic attachment and the psychogenesis of post-traumatic stress disorder. *Australian and New Zealand Journal of Psychiatry*, 36: 9–30.

Schore, A. N. (2003). *Affect Dysregulation and Disorders of the Self*. New York: Norton.

Sequiera, H., & Hollins, S. (2003). Clinical effects of sexual abuse on people with learning disability. Critical literature review. *British Journal of Psychiatry*, 182: 13–19.

Sinason, V. (1992). *Mental Handicap and the Human Condition*. London: Free Association.

Sinason, V. (Ed.) (2002a). *Attachment, Trauma and Multiplicity: Working with Dissociative Identity Disorder*. London: Routledge.

Sinason, V. (2002b). Treating people with learning disability after physical or sexual abuse. *Advances in Psychiatric Treatment*, 8: 424–432.

Skuse, D., Bentovim, A., Hodges, J., Stevenson, J., Andreou, C., Lanyado, M., New, M., Williams, B., & McMillan, D. (1998). Risk factors for development of sexually abusive behaviour in sexually victimised adolescent boys: cross sectional study. *British Medical Journal*, 317: 175–179.

Smith, J. (2007). From base evidence through to evidence base; a consideration of the NICE guidelines. *Psychoanalytic Psychotherapy*, 21(1): 40–60.

Sobsey, D. (1994). *Violence and Abuse in the Lives of People with Disabilities. The End of Silent Acceptance?* Baltimore, MD: Paul H Brookes.

Sobsey, D., & Varnhagen, C. (1989). Sexual abuse and exploitation of people with disabilities: towards prevention and treatment. In: M. Wapo & L. Gougen (Eds.), *Special Education across Canada*. Vancouver: Centre for Human Development and Research.

Sobsey, D., Grey, S., Wells, D., Pyper, D., & Reimer-Heck, B. (1991). *Disability, Sexuality and Abuse, An Annotated Bibliography*. Baltimore, MD: Paul H Brookes.

Solms, M., & Turnbull, O. (2002). *The Brain and the Inner World*. New York: Other Books.

Spataro, J., Mullen, P. E., Burgess, P. M., Wells, D. L., & Moss, S. A. (2004). Impact of child sexual abuse on mental health; Prospective study in males and females. *British Journal of Psychiatry*, 184: 416–421.

Spitz, R. A. (1945). Hospitalism—an inquiry into the genesis of psychiatric conditions in early childhood. *Psychoanalytic Study of the Child*,

1: 53–74 [reprinted in: R. N. Emde (Ed.), *Dialogues from Infancy*. New York: International Universities Press, 1983].

Sroufe, L. A., Egeland, B., Carlson, E. A., & Collins, W. A. (2005). *The Development of the Person. The Minnesota Study of Risk and Adaptation from Birth to Adulthood*. New York: Guilford.

Starr, R. H., Dietrich, K. N., Fischoff, J., Ceresnie, S., & Zweier, D. (1984). The contribution of handicapping conditions to child abuse. *Topics Early Childhood Special Education*, 1: 55–59.

Stern, D. (1985). *The Interpersonal World of the Infant: A View from Psychoanalysis and Developmental Psychology*. New York: Basic Books.

Sternfeld, L. (1977). Report of the medical director to the members of the corporation. UCPA Annual Conference, Washington, DC.

Stobart, E. (2006). *Child Abuse Linked to Accusations of "Possession" and "Witchcraft"*. Research Report RR750. London: Department for Education and Skills. http://www.dfes.gov.uk/research/data/uploadfiles/RR750.pdf

Strauss, M. (2001). Prevalence of violence against dating partners by male and female university students worldwide. *Violence Against Women*, 10(7): 790–811.

Strauss, M. A. (1993). Physical assaults by wives: a major social problem. In: R. J. Gelles & D. R. Loseke (Eds.), *Current Controversies on Family Violence* (pp. 67–87). Newbury Park, CA: Sage.

Sullivan, P. M., & Scanlan, J. M. (1988). Abuse issues with handicapped children. Paper presented at the National Symposium on Child Abuse, San Diego.

Sullivan, P. M., Vernon, M., & Scanlan, J. M. (1987). Sexual abuse and deaf youth. *American Annals of the Deaf*, 132(4): 256–262.

Sutton Smith, D. (Ed.) (1992). *Groups for Incest Survivors: A Handbook Based on Practice at the Women's Therapy Centre*. London: Women's Therapy Centre.

Target, M. (1998). The recovered memories controversy. *International Journal of Psychoanalysis*, 79: 1015–1028.

Target, M., & Fonagy, P. (2005). The psychological treatment of child and adolescent psychiatric disorders. In: A. Roth & P. Fonagy (Eds.), *What Works for Whom? A Critical Review of Psychotherapy Research* (2nd edn) (pp. 385–424). New York: Guilford.

Teicher, M. H., Samson, J. A., Polcari, A., & McGreenery, C. E. (2006). Sticks, stones, and hurtful words: relative effects of various forms of child maltreatment. *American Journal of Psychiatry*, 163(6): 993–1000.

The Survivors' Trust: www.thesurvivorstrust.org

Trickett, P. K., Noll, J. G., Reiffman, A., & Putnam, F. W. (2001). Variants of intrafamilial sexual abuse experience: implications for short and long-term development. *Development and Psychopathology, 13*: 1001–1019.

Trowell, J., Kolvin, I., Weeramanthri, T., Sadowski, H., Berelowitz, M., Glasser, D., & Leitch, I. (2002). Psychotherapy for sexually abused girls: psychopathological outcome findings and patterns of change. *British Journal of Psychiatry, 180*: 234–247.

Tutkun, H., Sar, V., Yargic, L. I., Ozpulat, T., Yanik, M., & Kiziltan, E. (1998). Frequency of dissociative disorders among psychiatric inpatients in a Turkish university clinic. *American Journal of Psychiatry,155*: 800–805.

University of Minnesota. *The Minnesota Longitudinal Study of Parents and Children.* www.cehd.umn.edu/ICD/Parent-Child/default.html

van der Hart, O., Nijenhuis, E. R. S., & Steele K. (2006). *The Haunted Self. Structural Dissociation and the Treatment of Chronic Traumatization.* New York: Norton.

van der Kolk, B. A. (1996). The body keeps the score. Approaches to the psychobiology of posttraumatic stress disorder. In: B. A. van der Kolk, A. C. McFarlane, & L. Weisaeth (Eds.), *Traumatic Stress. The Effects of Overwhelming Experience on Mind, Body and Society* (pp. 417–440). New York: Guilford.

van der Kolk, B. A., Roth, S., Pelcovitz, D., Sunday, S., & Spinazzola, J. (2005). Editorial: Disorders of extreme stress: the empirical foundation of a complex adaptation to trauma. *Journal of Traumatic Stress, 18*(5): 389.

van Ijzendoorn, M. H., Schuengel, C., & Bakermans-Kranenburg, M. J. (1999). Disorganized attachment in early childhood: meta-analysis of precursors, concomitants, and sequelae. *Developmental Psychopathology, 11*: 225–249.

Valenti-Hein, D., & Schwartz, L. (1995). *The Sexual Abuse Interview for those with Developmental Disabilities.* Santa Barbara, CA: James Stanfield.

Vize, C. M., & Cooper, P. J. (1995). Sexual abuse in patients with eating disorder, patients with depression, and normal controls, a comparative study. *British Journal of Psychiatry, 167*: 80–85.

Walby, S., & Allen, J. (2004). *Inter-Personal Violence: Findings from the 2001 British Crime Survey.* London: Home Office.

Waller, N. G., & Ross, C. A. (1997). The prevalence and biometric structure of pathological dissociation in the general population:

taxometric and behavioral genetic findings. *Journal of Abnormal Psychology, 106*: 499–510.

Warren, F., & Dolan, B. (Eds.) (2001). *Perspectives on the Henderson Hospital* (2nd edn). Sutton: Henderson Hospital.

Welldon, E. (1988). *Mother, Madonna, Whore. The Idealization and Denigration of Motherhood*. London: Karnac.

Westcott, H. (1991). The abuse of disabled children: a review of the literature. *Child: Care, Health and Development, 17*: 243–258.

Whitaker, D. J., Haileyesus, T., Swahn, M., & Saltzman, L. S. (2007). Differences in frequency of violence and reported injury between relationships with reciprocal and nonreciprocal intimate partner violence. *American Journal of Public Health, 97*(5): 941–947.

Widom, C. P. (1989). The cycle of violence. *American Association for the Advancement of Science, 244*: 160–166.

Widom, C. S. (1989). Child abuse, neglect, and adult behavior: research design and findings on criminality, violence, and child abuse. *American Journal of Orthopsychiatry, 59*: 355–367.

Wilkinson, M. A. (2006). *Coming into Mind. The Mind–Brain Relationship: A Jungian Clinical Perspective*. Hove: Brunner-Routledge.

Wilkinson, M. A. (2009). *Change in the Consulting-room*. New York: Norton (in press).

Williams, G. P. (2004). Response to B. Proner's paper "Bodily states of anxiety. The movement from somatic states to thoughtfulness and relatedness", given at the Scientific Meeting of the Society of Analytical Psychology, London, 4 October.

Women's Therapy Centre (2005). *Discovering Bits and Pieces of Me: Women's Experiences of Psychoanalytical Psychotherapy*. www.womenstherapycentre.co.uk

World Health Organization (1992). *The International Classification of Diseases (ICD-10): Classification of Mental and Behavioural Disorders: Clinical Descriptions and Diagnostic Guidelines* (10th revision). Geneva: World Health Organization.

Zirpoli, T. J. (1990). Physical abuse: are children with disabilities at greater risk? *Intervention in School and Clinic, 26*: 6–11.

INDEX

at risk children
  chronically ill, 25
  deaf, 25–26
  disabled, 25–26 *see also*: learning
    disabilities
  in the care system, 25
  previously abused, 25
  refugee and asylum seeking, 25
  socially excluded family, 25
attachment(s), 30
  adult interview, 45
  and mental illness, 50
  and trauma, 46, 50–51
  disorders/difficulty, 2, 6, 8, 44,
    70, 72
  experiences, 78–79
  figures/relationships/bonds, 16,
    44–45, 47, 78–79, 81
  measurement and classification,
    64
  styles, 45, 79, 81
    infants' "strange situation"
      behaviour, 45–47
    insecure anxious/ambivalent,
      46–47
    insecure/avoidant, 46–47
    insecure disorganized, 46–47,
      49–50, 53, 76, 81 *see also*:
      trauma; post traumatic stress
      disorder
    secure, 46–47, 50–51, 76, 79
  theory, 32, 44, 80
  therapeutic, 77, 79
  traumatic, 50
avoidant coping, 17 *see also*:
    attachment style; child abuse,
    effects in childhood

Baer, L., 52, 104
Bajer, W. L., 48, 111
Baker, A. W., 12, 98
Bakermans-Kranenburg, M. J., 47,
    115
Barkman, K., 52, 112
Barling, J., 41, 100
Bateman, A., 69–70, 98, 103

Bauserman, R., 12, 14, 43, 111
Beardsall, L., 43, 105
Beardslee, W. R., 18, 108
Beecham, J., 70, 98
behaviour(s), 3, 7–8, 15, 22, 29, 52,
    54, 81
  aggressive, 30
  attachment, 45–46
    disorganized, 47
    insecure, 47
  hypervigilant, 28
  problems, 60
  proximity-seeking, 44–45
  risk/health risk, 19
    obesity, 19
    sexual
      promiscuity/prostitution, 19
      sexually transmitted infection,
        19
    smoking/substance abuse, 19
    teenage pregnancy, 19 *see also*:
      child abuse, effects in
      adulthood
  self-destructive/impulsive, 54
  self-harming, 30
  sexualized, 17, 32, 39, 61 *see also*:
    child abuse, effects in
    childhood
  sexually abusive (juvenile), 44
  sexually harmful, 17
  strange situation, 45–46
  suicidal, 17
  violent/abusive, 4
Belaise, C., 19, 111
Bentovim, A., 12, 17, 43, 98, 109, 113
Berelowitz, M., 67, 115
Berkowitz, R., 52, 112
Berliner, L., 17, 103
Bernatzky, G., 77, 110
Bifulco, A., 18, 98
Birmingham Rape and Sexual
    Violence Project *see* survivor
    organizations
Black, N., 65, 98
black/Asian/ethnic minority
    groups, 41, 55, 75, 92–93